Preface

Guides to the historic monuments of Northern Irela
since 1926. So this guide is part of a long tradition
historic environment available to the public in a form that is ___
The previous guide was last updated in 1983, and has been out of print for several years.

With new acquisitions of historic monuments, and with advances in our understanding
of these sites, this new guide is a welcome addition to the suite of internationally-
recognised, award-winning publications commissioned by the Built Heritage Directorate
of the Northern Ireland Environment Agency and its predecessors.

Northern Ireland's historic monuments form a key part of our historic environment. They
are places that everyone can enjoy, and sites where everyone should feel welcome.
They are also key destinations for tourists in Northern Ireland, whether from overseas or
locals, and whether individuals, families or groups.

The Northern Ireland Environment Agency is committed to making the information that
it holds about the historic environment accessible to the wider public, and this guide is a
significant step forward in achieving that goal.

Most of this guide has been compiled by Marion Meek, a former Senior Inspector of
Historic Monuments, who worked for many years on the conservation of these sites and
their presentation to the public. Marion is to be commended for her enthusiasm and
commitment to the built heritage in general and I wish to offer my personal thanks for
her help in preparing this guide.

Michael D.A. Coulter
Director, Built Heritage
Spring 2009

Introductory Note

What is an historic monument? It is hard to give an answer that covers all of the sites that are listed in this guide. Some historic monuments are grand structures, surviving today as imposing cliff-top ruins, mysterious settings of stones or great earthworks. But not every historic monument is a big or ancient structure. Some were everyday places where ordinary things happened – places that were used as farmsteads, sites of industry or places of worship. Some of the sites listed in this book are amongst the oldest structures to survive in the modern landscape, such as elaborate stone tombs that are over 5,000 years old. There are sites from much more recent times, including the Martello Tower at Magilligan, built in 1812, and the defence heritage site of Grey Point Fort, established in 1907.

All of the historic monuments recorded in this guide are buildings or structures that were made and used in the past, and they are all important reservoirs of information about societies that once lived here. They are places where one can literally touch the past – places that were built or used hundreds or thousands of years ago.

The Historic Monuments and Archaeological Objects (Northern Ireland) Order 1995 is the main piece of legislation that provides statutory protection for our archaeological assets. This legislation enables the Northern Ireland Environment Agency (an Agency within the Department of Environment) to care for, and present to the public, an array of historic monuments that are representative of the rich archaeological heritage that has survived here. The historic monuments recorded in this guide are in state care, cared for by the Northern Ireland Environment Agency, and most of these are open to the public. There are many more monuments in private ownership, as well as monuments owned by other bodies such as the National Trust and local councils.

This guide book was last updated in 1983, and since then the Department of the Environment has acquired more monuments that are now cared for and presented to the public. There has also been significant growth in knowledge about our archaeology, especially with developer-funded archaeological investigations in advance of new infrastructural and other built development. The descriptions of the monuments contained in this book give information about their location (using Irish Grid References), how to get to them, and some references to previously published accounts. The descriptions also make extensive use of official archive reports gathered and maintained by the Northern Ireland Environment Agency.

In all cases, the Northern Ireland Environment Agency seeks to ensure that our historic monuments are treated with respect and care. These are unique sites, to be enjoyed by present generations while ensuring that future generations will also have a built heritage to learn from and enjoy. It is hoped that readers will use this guide as an introduction to Northern Ireland's rich archaeological heritage, and be encouraged to go out and explore this diverse resource. Most (but not all) of the historic monuments described in this guide can be accessed by the visiting public. Access to the majority of the monuments is free of charge, and there are many events organised throughout the year that are open to the public. For further details of these, please access our website at www.ni-environment.gov.uk.

Dr John D.J. O'Keeffe
Principal Inspector of Historic Monuments

How the Guide is Laid Out

This guide is laid out in six main sections that cover each of the counties in Northern Ireland. A fold-out map is included at the back cover that shows the location of the monuments described. The monuments are identified by a number, and this number is used in the main text starting at 1. Ballylumford Dolmen and ending with 190. Carrignahaltora.

Each of the counties is colour-coded for ease of reference in the guide, and each section begins with a more detailed map that shows the location of the monuments described. The approximate distance of the monuments from the nearest towns or villages is provided in both imperial and metric measurements. Grid references used throughout the text are Irish Grid References, and can be easily used with the 1:50,000 Discovery Series Ordnance Survey maps. References to published material relating to the monuments are given at the end of entries as appropriate.

Illustrations have been provided for most of the monuments, usually as photographs of the sites described. The Northern Ireland Environment Agency is presently updating signage, on a rolling programme, at these monuments, and developing further visitor information in the form of site-specific leaflets and booklets. Unfortunately it is not possible in a book of this nature to include a detailed plan of all the monuments or references to all of the published material that relates to them. A bibliography is provided for the reader at the end of the guide should they wish to find out more about a particular site.

Contents

County Antrim   2

County Armagh   24

County Down   42

County Fermanagh   80

County Londonderry   94

County Tyrone   114

Bibliography/Abbreviations used in the inventory   140

County Antrim

PREHISTORIC MONUMENTS

1. Ballylumford Dolmen (D431016)
2. Craigs, The Broad Stone (C979175)
3. Craigs Dolmen (C974173)
4. Dooey's Cairn (D021182)
5. Duncarbit Standing Stones (D147347)
6. Lissanduff Earthworks (C930422)
7. Ossian's Grave (or Cloghbrack) (D213284)

EARLY CHRISTIAN PERIOD MONUMENTS

8. Antrim Round Tower (JI54878)
9. Armoy Round Tower (D078332)
10. Ballywee Enclosed Farmstead (J218899)
11. Coshkib Rath Pair: The Twin Towers (D234292)
12. Drumnadrough Rath (J330812)
13. Lissue Rath (J228633)
14. Spring Farm Rath (J149882)

MEDIEVAL MONUMENTS

15. Bonamargy Friary (DI26408)
16. Carrickfergus Castle (J415873)
17. Castle Lug (J375844)
18. Cranfield Church (J055853)
19. Dunluce Castle (C904414)
20. Harryville Motte and Bailey (D112026)
21. Kinbane Castle (DO88439)
22. Layd Church (D245289)
23. Muckamore Priory (JI67854)
24. Olderfleet Castle (D413016)

PLANTATION PERIOD AND LATER MONUMENTS

25. Carrickfergus Town Walls (J415876 and area)
26. Carrickfergus Gasworks (J410873)
27. Dalway's Bawn (J443914)
28. Moira Station House and Signal-Box (J158618)

County Antrim
Prehistoric Monuments

1 Ballylumford Dolmen (D431016)

Location: Close to the north-west tip of Islandmagee, reached by the B90 road (off the A2 coast road) from Larne. Now somewhat unexpectedly in the front garden of a listed, mid 19th-century house and popularly known as the Druid's Altar, this may be a portal tomb, a Neolithic burial monument now denuded of its cairn, or the remains of a passage tomb.

PSAMNI 1940, 35; Brett 1996, 5.

Ballylumford Dolmen

2 Craigs, The Broad Stone (C979175)

Location: 3 miles (4.8km) north of Rasharkin, on the west side of Long Mountain, approached from the north-west on a good road through rough, boggy upland (a long walk). A shallow forecourt leads to three chambers in a long, stone-revetted cairn. Despite the superficial appearance of a 'dolmen', created by propping a large capstone on the portals in recent times, this is a well-preserved court tomb. Craigs Dolmen (**3**) is a mile to the south-west.

Evans 1966, 44–45

Craigs, The Broad Stone

3 Craigs Dolmen (C974173)

Location: 2³/₄ miles (4.4km) north of Rasharkin, on a level terrace on the west side of Long Mountain, in a field west of a minor road. Eight closely-set upright stones form a chamber and there are indications of a passage. According to an 1883 description, an earthen mound formerly covered the stones. In the winter of 1976–1977 frost shattered the basalt capstone into five

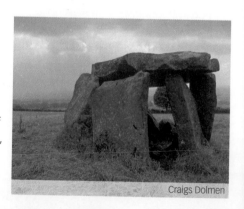
Craigs Dolmen

pieces. After the monument was placed in state care the cap was mended with steel bars and stone adhesive, and a small excavation was done to provide information before its re-erection. These are clearly the remains of a Neolithic passage tomb, though the earlier finding of a 'cinerary urn' and a mid second-millennium BC radiocarbon date point to Bronze Age activity. The Broad Stone (2) is a mile to the north-east.

B.B. Williams in *Ulster J. Archaeol.* 50 (1987), 129–133

4 Dooey's Cairn (D021182)

Dooey's Cairn

Location: ³/₄ mile (1.2km) south-south-east of Dunloy in Ballymacaldrack townland, reached by a side road west off the B93. This well-known court tomb was excavated in 1935 by Estyn Evans and again in 1975 by Pat Collins, and is dated using radiocarbon to between 3000 and 2500 BC. A U-shaped forecourt leads to a stone chamber with, beyond, a long 'cremation passage' with three circular pits, which originally held wooden posts. The cairn's edges are revetted with stone. The excavations indicated several stages of use and Gabriel Cooney has suggested a four-phase sequence of construction and use. There are many similarities between this monument and excavated sites in southern Scotland. With the two Craigs tombs, this forms an interesting group of Neolithic burial monuments on Long Mountain.

E.E. Evans in *Ulster J. Archaeol.* 1 (1938), 59–68; A.E.P. Collins in *Ulster J. Archaeol.* 39 (1976), 1–7; Herity 1987, esp. 164–168 and figs 13–14; Cooney 2000, 99–103

5 Duncarbit Standing Stones (D147347)

Duncarbit Standing Stones

Location: A quarter of a mile (0.5km) south-east of Killuca Bridge, reached by a long, rough, undefined route. Two tall, slender standing stones may be the remains of a once more extensive stone alignment. Local name 'Slaght' suggests burial traditions and the stones are believed to mark the burial place of John Roe MacDonnell, killed while fleeing from the battle of Gleshesk in 1567.

6 Lissanduff Earthworks (C930422)

Location: On high ground north-east of Portballintrae, where the River Bush approaches the sea, in Bushfoot or Lissanduff townland, reached by a footpath uphill from the car park on the shore. There are two large earthworks, each with a central enclosure and a surrounding bank, and with a wide space between these banks. The smaller (north-east)

Lissanduff Earthworks

enclosure is incomplete along its north-west edge where a large early 19th-century house once stood, and an outhouse still survives on the line of the inner bank. Both enclosing banks are circular and are high, the inner face of the inner one being particularly steep, in places revetted with brick from the use of the area as a garden in the 19th century. The larger (south-west) earthwork has a roughly circular inner enclosure surrounded by an irregularly oval outer bank. The whole area is damp but, in particular, the inner enclosure was built around a natural spring. Both the date and the purpose of this site remain a puzzle. The earthworks are certainly not 'ordinary' raths and it is tempting to suggest a ritual function associated with the spring and a prehistoric date (compare Coshkib (**11**) and the King's Stables (**36**)), but further research is needed to unlock the secrets of these enigmatic enclosures. Ordnance Survey officers noted them in the 1830s and reported the local name, the 'Cups and Saucers', but since then the monument seems to have escaped notice in publications.

Day and McWilliams 1992, 106 and 116

7 Ossian's Grave (or Cloghbrack) (D213284)

Location: In Lubitavish townland, 1³/₄ miles (2.8km) west-north-west of Cushendall, approached on the A2 road to Cushendun, then after about 1¹/₂ miles by a minor road to the west, and a track south off this. Park at the foot of the hill and walk up the lane to the monument, a hillside court tomb with fine views to Glendun, Glenaan and Scotland. A semicircular forecourt opens into a two-chambered burial gallery, formerly set in a short oval cairn. Although romantically named after Ossian, the Early Christian period warrior-poet, it is a Neolithic tomb. The poet, John Hewitt, loved this site and a stone in his memory stands near the tomb.

PSAMNI 1940, 19

Ossian's Grave (or Cloghbrack)

County Antrim
Early Christian Period Monuments

8 Antrim Round Tower (JI54878)

Location: North of the town in Steeple townland, in the landscaped grounds of Steeple House, the former Antrim Borough Council Offices. Though the tower now stands among lawns and trees, it was once surrounded by buildings. Antrim was an important early ecclesiastical site, probably a 6th-century foundation, closely connected with Bangor. The round tower is some 28m high and is built of roughly-coursed basalt rubble. It has the familiar raised door but, unusually, there is a cross-carved stone above the lintel. There are eight simple windows, including four at the top below the cap. A 10th-century date is likely. The interior is not accessible at present. This is one of only two complete round towers in Northern Ireland; the other is on Devenish (112). The 'Witch's Stone' nearby has two hollows on its surface and is a form of bullaun stone.

Antrim Round Tower

Ordnance Survey Memoir for the Parish of Antrim (Public Record Office of Northern Ireland, 1969), 74–78; Gwynn and Hadcock 1970, 28; Brett 1996, 6; Lalor 1999, 100–103

9 Armoy Round Tower (D078332)

Location: About half a mile (0.8km) east of Armoy village, reached by turning off the A44, in Glebe townland, the tower is in the graveyard of Armoy Church of Ireland parish church. There is a lay-by at the church. The road curves round the graveyard, and a souterrain was found during road-widening here in the 1990s, both confirming Early Christian period activity at the site. More recent investigations (2004–2005) in advance of an extension to the graveyard also

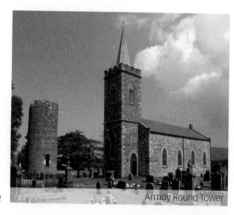
Armoy Round Tower

uncovered further evidence of Early Christian and medieval activity at the site, including the discovery of another souterrain. The early church was associated with Bishop Olcan, placed here according to late tradition by St Patrick. Later it was the site of the medieval parish church. The tower is incomplete, surviving to a height of 10.8m. It was once taller, but nothing like the height of Antrim tower (8). The stone is mainly sandstone, roughly-dressed and coursed, with long, narrow slabs below and more rounded boulders above. The topmost courses were rebuilt in the 19th century when the tower was reused as a belfry. There are no surviving windows. The door is unusually tall and narrow, with a semicircular head and outlining raised band. The door sill is now only about 1.6m above ground level, but this has risen considerably because of burials and the door was originally much further from the ground. During recent conservation work new jamb stones were built into the door to replace rough brick and rubble patching. The tower must date from the 11th or 12th century. The parish church was built largely in 1820 and 1846, but it occupied the site of an earlier church, partly uncovered in a small excavation in 1997.

E. Getty in *Ulster J. Archaeol.* 4 (1856), 173–177; S.K. Kirker in *J. Roy. Soc. Antiq. Ireland* 29 (1899), 121–125; Brett 1996, 7; Lalor 1999, 102–103; CAF, DSR No. 44

10 Ballywee Enclosed Farmstead (J218899)

Ballywee Enclosed Farmstead

Location: 4½ miles (7.2km) east-north-east of Antrim, and 2 miles (3.2km) north of Parkgate, on the east slopes of Donegore Hill. This complex settlement was threatened with levelling but was excavated by C.J. Lynn in 1974 and is now preserved in state care. A low, discontinuous bank encloses a roughly figure-of-eight-shaped area, but on this wet hill slope, the bank was partly to deflect water as well as for defence. Nine Early Christian period structures were excavated including a rectangular house with a hearth, attached souterrain and outhouse, two other souterrains, another outbuilding and traces of further buildings. The three souterrains suggest that security was a consideration for a prosperous society. A spring-fed stream ran down the middle of the enclosure. This is an unusually well-preserved secular settlement, a variation on more familiar raths and cashels so common in Co. Antrim.

PoP 1988, 32–35

County Antrim
Early Christian Period Monuments

11 Coshkib Rath Pair: The Twin Towers (D234292)

Location: 1 mile (1.6km) north of Cushendall, beautifully sited at over 500 feet (160m), overlooking sea and glens. Two circular embanked enclosures close together, one with a waterlogged interior. These may not be 'ordinary' Early Christian farmstead enclosures (see Lissanduff (6)) but their nature is uncertain without excavation. No established access.

Coshkib Rath Pair: The Twin Towers

12 Drumnadrough Rath (J330812)

Location: In north Belfast, approached by the Whitewell Road and the turning into Fairy Knowe Drive, near the junction with Floral Road. This platform rath occupies a small eminence on the north-east-facing hillside, below the Zoological Gardens. Its surroundings are greatly altered, by the M2 motorway in a deep cutting on the north-east and modern houses on the other sides. In earlier years it survived in the garden of a big house called Fairy Knowe. The rath is still known as the Fairy Knowe, perhaps a name that comes from the eminence on which it stands or an earlier folklore tradition about the site. The platform is well preserved, except on the east where it was encroached on by the garden. The north-south diameter is 39m and the platform is up to 1.1m above the surroundings. A low bank can be traced around the edge of the platform. The interior is known to have been disturbed in the past when the area was farmed. This may be the last survivor of a ring of raths, which once existed on the lower hill slopes in north and west Belfast so, despite the altered surroundings, it is a precious reminder of a monument type which was once common in these now built-up areas of the city.

13 Lissue Rath (J228633)

Location: North of the A3 road between Lisburn and Moira, reached from a minor road at Englishtown. The surroundings of the site are greatly altered as it is now surrounded by an industrial estate. Excavation by Professor Gerhart Bersu in 1946–1947 showed that the circular banked and ditched enclosure, superficially unimpressive, was a complex Early Christian farmstead. Its diameter is big, at about 60m, and excavation showed that the present site had been preceded by a smaller enclosure. Its wet ditch produced many organic finds, including wooden bowls and a churn. The second earthwork, the one now visible, had three phases and in each the whole interior was occupied by a single, huge building with a central hearth. Nothing like this has been found elsewhere and it has been suggested that it was a royal site.

G. Bersu in *Ulster J. Archaeol.* 11 (1948), 131–133; Evans 1966, 48–49; R. Warner in *Lisburn Hist. Soc. J.* 6 (1986–1987), 28–36

14 Spring Farm Rath (J149882)

Spring Farm Rath

Location: 1 mile (1.6km) north of Antrim, south of Stiles Way in Spring Farm estate. A well-preserved platform rath, sited on fairly level ground rising gently to the north-east. The platform, 30m in diameter, is surrounded by a partly waterlogged ditch, 1m deep but originally much deeper. This was the homestead of a farming family in the Early Christian period, but traces of their house and farm buildings could only be recovered by excavation. The rath is an attractive landmark and an island of green among recent houses, a reminder of farmers in the area a thousand years ago.

County Antrim
Medieval Monuments

15 Bonamargy Friary (DI26408)

Bonamargy Friary

Location: half a mile (0.8km) east of
Ballycastle, south of the A2 to Cushendun
in Ballycastle golf course. Small car park at
entrance. This Third Order Franciscan Friary,
traditionally founded by Rory MacQuillan in
about 1500, was involved in warfare in the
late 16th century, but was repaired and used
until the mid 17th century. The approach is
through a gatehouse set in an earth bank,
a rare survival. The long narrow church
has three windows and a door in the south wall and a two-phase east window with
broken flamboyant tracery. North of the church was a cloister and in the east range is
the sacristy for storing equipment, a day-room for indoor work and the friars' dormitory
above. The 17th-century chapel and vault running south from the church hold the burial
place of the MacDonnells, Earls of Antrim. There are many interesting gravestones in the
surrounding cemetery, including memorials for sailors of the two world wars drowned off
the nearby coast.

F.J. Bigger and W.J. Fennell in *Ulster J. Archaeol.* special volume (1898); Gwynn and
Hadcock 1970, 269; Brett 1996, 15; J. Bell and T.E. McNeill in *Ulster J. Archaeol.*, vol. 16
(2002) 98–116

16 Carrickfergus Castle (J415873)

Carrickfergus Castle

Location: At the west approach to
Carrickfergus on the coast road (A2) from
Belfast. Large car park nearby. Strategically
sited on a rocky promontory to command
Belfast Lough. Begun by John de Courcy
soon after his 1177 invasion of Ulster, the
castle played an important military role until
1928. Its long history includes sieges by King
John in 1210 and Edward Bruce in 1315, its
capture by Schomberg for William III in 1689,
and capture by the French under Thurot in
1760. The castle was used by the army until
1928, and in the 1939–1945 war it housed
air-raid shelters.

Carrickfergus Castle

Earliest is the polygonal inner ward on the tip of the rock, begun in about 1178, built in one programme with the great keep. The middle ward was added between 1217 and 1222 with a postern gate to the sea and the east tower with its cross-bow loops at near water level. The outer ward and gatehouse were probably built between 1226 and 1242, taking in the full extent of the rocky promontory. The gatehouse, traditionally the residence of the constable of the castle, includes on the east side a chapel and in the centre, over the gate, the windlass for the portcullis. Later changes were mainly concerned with provision for guns and the castle's use as an ordnance depot. Cannon from the 17th to 19th centuries are on show and the keep houses historical and other displays.

McNeill 1981; DOENI guide-card (1992); Donnelly 1997, 81–82; Ó Baoill, 2008

County Antrim
Medieval Monuments

17 Castle Lug (J375844)

Castle Lug

Location: 3 miles (4.8km) south-west of Carrickfergus, in West Division townland, on the inland side of the A2 coast road at Greenisland. Small lay-by beside the busy road. Known also as Cloughnalarty and Cloughlougherty, the castle is a fragment of a late medieval tower-house on a small height overlooking Belfast Lough. Only the north wall and traces of the north-east corner survive, and though a square plan has been suggested a small excavation in 1980 showed that no traces remained of the other walls. The masonry is mainly local basalt and the main feature of the north wall is a break rising through almost its whole height, possibly the remains of a window or fireplace. A mid 16th-century date is likely, but it was reported as ruined in the early 17th century. A link with the Lug (Lugg) family, prominent in Carrickfergus in the 16th and 17th centuries, is possible but cannot be proved. This sad fragment of a tower-house now stands among modern houses, but its situation, just east of the Silver Stream, points to its importance in the 16th century, protecting the coastal route into the old borough or 'county' of Carrickfergus from the south-east.

N.F. Brannon in *Ulster J. Archaeol.* 44–45 (1981–1982), 202–203

18 Cranfield Church (J055853)

Cranfield Church

Location: Beautifully set beside Lough Neagh, on a small rise at Churchtown Point, 3³/₄ miles (6km) south-west of Randalstown and 5 miles (8km) south-east of Toome. Large car park at lough shore. This small ruined church in its graveyard was the medieval parish church, probably abandoned in the 17th century. The ruin is simple and difficult to date but may be 13th century. A wooden cross inside is a replica of an ancient timber termon cross, formerly north of the church, marking the boundary of church lands. Nearby on the shore to the east is a famous holy well, traditionally associated with St Colman and still a focus for pilgrims, especially in May and June. The well is the site of an annual Mass, which includes the blessing of Lough Neagh fishermen's boats.

F.J. Bigger and W.J. Fennell in *Ulster J. Archaeol.* 4 (1897), 48–49; Brett 1996, 13

19 Dunluce Castle (C904414)

Location: Spectacularly sited beside the coast road (A2) between Portrush and Bushmills. The image of the castle on the cliffs is familiar from book covers, calendars and occasional television appearances. Car park at entrance. The *dún* name and rock-cut souterrain suggest Early Christian period occupation on the rocky headland. The earliest parts of the castle may date from the 14th century but it is not documented until the 16th, when it was in the hands of MacQuillans and later MacDonnells. Badly damaged in an artillery attack by the English Deputy, Sir John Perrott, in 1584, the castle was repaired by Sorley Boy and James MacDonnell, and extended by Randal MacDonnell after 1636. After a stormy history it decayed from the later 17th century onwards.

Dunluce Castle

The rectangular mainland court with ruined 17th-century domestic and service buildings leads downhill to the 'funnel', converging walls to channel people or stock towards the gap, now crossed by a fixed wooden bridge over a narrow 17th-century stone arch, but perhaps formerly by a drawbridge. The gatehouse with its corbelled-out turrets is of about 1600 and is Scottish in style. Apart possibly from the circular north-east and south-east towers and parts of the curtain walls, most of the buildings on the rock date from the 16th and early 17th centuries. Close to the south curtain wall a row of column bases is the remnant of an Italian-style *loggia* or covered way, based probably on a Scottish model, and belonging to the courtyard of an earlier, smaller hall. Dominating the yard is the two-storey hall range with its ruined bay windows, built by Randal MacDonnell, 2nd Earl of Antrim, after 1636. One window has been restored. Beyond were service rooms, a kitchen and a lower yard with domestic ranges. Much original paving and cobbling survives in the castle.

In the field west of the mainland court, the earthwork remains of a walled garden can be seen which is known to have included a bowling green. Beyond that are the extensive earthworks of Dunluce Town. To the south of the castle are the ruins of the town church with several interesting gravestones. Traditionally this was the last resting place of some of the people shipwrecked nearby in the Spanish Armada ship the Girona.

DOENI guide book 1993; DOENI guide-card 1997; Donnelly 1997, 97–99

20 Harryville Motte and Bailey (D112026)

Location: Prominently sited on the north bank of the River Braid on the south outskirts of Ballymena in Ballykeel townland. This is a fine earthwork castle, presumably of the late 12th or early 13th century, the biggest of a group in the Ballymena area. McNeill suggests that it was built by the O'Flynns rather than the Anglo-Normans because it lies outside the earldom. There is a large motte and a rectangular bailey to the east.

PSAMNI 1940, 30; Mallory and McNeill 1991, 269

Harryville Motte and Bailey

21 Kinbane Castle (D088439)

Location: In Cregganboy townland, 2½ miles (4km) north-west of Ballycastle, reached by a side turning north off the B15. From a large cliff-top car park a steep path leads to the shore, across a stony beach and up to the castle. This is dramatically sited on the *ceann bán*, the white (chalk) headland, in a position of great natural strength. Reported to have been built by Colla MacDonnell shortly before 1551, it is known to have been captured and partly destroyed by the English in that year, but was reoccupied and traditionally

Kinbane Castle

used until the mid 18th century. The castle was entered through a gate in the south wall, protected by a tower with a gun-loop at the south-west angle, partly ruined. The main surviving masonry is the tower at the south angle, two stories high with good detail visible. Beyond was a walled enclosure, partly defended by the steep cliffs and partly the wall, now largely grass-grown but with traces of at least two gun-loops north-east of the tower.

PLEASE NOTE: This site is dangerous because of eroding rock and steep drops. Great care is needed. The rock is not safe beyond the castle.

T.E. McNeill in *Ulster J. Archaeol.* 46 (1983), esp. 109–112

County Antrim
Medieval Monuments

22 Layd Church (D245289)

Location: In Moneyvart townland, 1 mile (1.6km) north-east of Cushendall, approached by a short footpath off the coast road to Torr Head. Car park at top of path. The ruined church in its graveyard is set beside a fast-flowing stream above the sea at Port Obe. Though there is a local tradition that it was a Franciscan foundation, this was a parish

Layd Church

church in 1302–1306 and continued in use until 1790. The fabric shows at least four phases of medieval and post-medieval remodelling. The long narrow church had a tower at the west end, with access to the upper floor by an external stair, probably to provide residential accommodation for the priest. Marks of wicker centring are clear under its vault. Fine gravestones in the yard include MacDonnell memorials and remind us of the area's maritime and Scottish connections. A holed cross stands near the graveyard gate, reused as a gravestone. The commonly found 'Layde' spelling of the name seems to be an antiquarian form, favoured by F.J. Bigger. The Ordnance Survey spelling of the parish is Layd.

F.J. Bigger and W.J. Fennell in *Ulster J. Archaeol.* 5 (1898), 35–46; *PSAMNI* 1940, 17–18; Brett 1996, 14

23 Muckamore Priory (JI67854)

Location: 1½ miles (2.4km) south-east of Antrim. Roadworks uncovered part of this priory of Augustinian Canons in 1973. It was founded by followers of John de Courcy before 1283 on the site of an earlier church and its dedication to SS Mary and Colman Elo acknowledges the earlier foundation. It is in state care awaiting further excavation and eventual display. The field is used as pasture and there are no visible remains.

Gwynn and Hadcock 1970, 188–189; *PoP* 1988, 72–75

24 Olderfleet Castle (D413016)

Location: On the shore of Larne harbour on the tongue of land called the Curran, now in built-up surroundings but once much more open to the sea. In several late 16th- and early 17th-century maps the waterway here is called Olderfleet Haven, but three castles are recorded around the harbour, *Coraine, Tchevet and Olderfleete*. From its position this ruin is likely to be Coraine, the other two having disappeared. The square, four-storey tower, badly ruined on the south, has pairs of double-splayed gun-loops in the basement and may have been a defended warehouse as well as controlling access to the harbour. There are no closely datable features but a 16th-century date is likely.

PSAMNI 1940, 33; E.M. Jope in *Ulster J. Archaeol.* 23 (1960), 100

Olderfleet Castle

County Antrim
Plantation Period and Later Monuments

25 Carrickfergus Town Walls (J415876 and area)

Location: In 1565 it was recognised that Carrickfergus was under threat as a symbol of the crown but Queen Elizabeth was unwilling to pay for town walls. A hundred men were put on the job, but work was slow and incomplete when, on 2 June 1573, Sir Brian Phelim O'Neill burnt the town. Work struggled on until Lord Deputy Sir Arthur Chichester took charge in 1599 and by 1610 had his fine mansion, Joymount, built in the east corner of the walled town.

Carrickfergus Town Walls

At least half of the town walls are still visible, often to the full height of 4m to the wall-walk. The wall extended from the castle north-west to Irish Gate, then north to North Gate, east to the rear of the Joymount property and south towards the water. The best-preserved stretch of wall, with the north-east corner bastion, can be seen from Shaftesbury Park next to the bowling green. Another good stretch, with a blocked 17th-century gate, can be seen along the east side of the library on the Joymount site. Other features include North Gate (dated 1608) at the end of North Street, twice restored in the 20th century but with some 17th-century stones still visible in the arch, and at the end of West Street, the footings of Irish Gate and the adjacent wall. This was excavated from 1977 to 1979 by the late T.G. Delaney, after whom the park, Delaney Green, is named.

The wall top is narrow and defence could only be by musket. Despite this, when the town was besieged by Schomberg's troops in 1689 it was able to hold out for a week before yielding to a superior force. The town was besieged again in 1760 by a French army under Thurot.

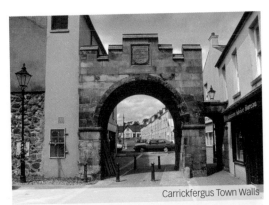
Carrickfergus Town Walls

PSAMNI 1940, 49; M.L. Simpson and A. Dickson in *Medieval Archaeology* 25 (1981), 78–89; Ó Baoill, 2008

26 Carrickfergus Gasworks (J410873)

Location: At the west edge of the town, in Irish Quarter South, just outside the town wall, easily identified from the tall gasholder. Carrickfergus Gasworks was recognised as being of great interest when all the old 'town gas' installations in Northern Ireland were under threat of closure and were surveyed in 1987. It survives as a remarkably complete example of a Victorian coal gas operation,

Carrickfergus Gasworks

unique in Ireland. It retained somewhat 'antique' technology that had been replaced long ago in most works, involving the use of horizontal retorts, and it has the largest surviving set of these in western Europe. All the stages in the process can be followed through the buildings and the machinery, and there is a display of gas appliances in what was the manager's house. The complex was acquired and taken into state care in 1982 and subsequently leased to the Carrickfergus Gasworks Preservation Society, a charitable company which conserves, manages and provides access to the public. Now that natural gas is widely available and taken for granted, it is important to preserve the memory of the manufacture and use of coal gas in the past

PLEASE NOTE: Access is limited. Please contact the Carrickfergus Tourist Information Centre for information.

McCutcheon 1980, pls 130–132

County Antrim
Plantation Period and Later Monuments

27 Dalway's Bawn (J443914)

Location: 3 miles (4.8km) north-east of Carrickfergus on the west side of the B90 road to Ballycarry in Ballyhill townland. A well-preserved example of an early 17th-century planter's fortified enclosure, built in about 1609 by John Dalway, constable of Carrickfergus Castle, to secure his royal grant of land in the area. Now enmeshed with a

Dalway's Bawn

working farm, only part of the bawn is in state care – the roadside wall and three flanker towers, viewable only from the road. A dwelling house formerly stood inside the bawn, but it was demolished in the 19th century.

A.T. Lee in *Ulster J. Archaeol.* 6 (1858), 125–132; *PSAMNI* 1940, 40; Brett 1996, 22; C. McGranaghan in *Ulster J. Archaeol.* 66 (2007) 132–138

28 Moira Station House and Signal-Box (J158618)

Location: Very close to the Co. Down boundary, in Magheramesk townland, about 1 mile (1.6km) north-north-east of Moira, approached along Station Road from the north-east outskirts of the village. Open access to the platforms, and the station house can be opened by appointment. Moira has Northern Ireland's oldest surviving railway station, built in 1841, only 11 years after the world's first passenger service opened between Manchester and Liverpool in 1830. The station house was designed in an Italianate style by the Ulster Railway's chief engineer, John Godwin, and is built of a mixture of stone, brick and stucco, with a slated roof, tall chimneys and distinctive round-headed doors and windows. It appears to be a single storey from the platform but is two storeys high at the back, with accommodation for the stationmaster at the lower level. Inside are waiting rooms, a ticket office, a luggage room, lavatories and access to the lower floor. The 1890 signal-box which stood at the level-crossing was moved to its present position when the crossing became automatic. In 1945 the station had 15 staff, there were yards for cattle

Moira Station House and Signal Box

and coal, and a siding to goods sheds. A new house for the stationmaster was built in the late 19th century. This, as well as the yards and goods sheds, are now the headquarters of the Northern Ireland Environment Agency's (NIEA's) historic monuments conservation workforce and its craft workshops. When the signals were automated in 1984 and the station became at that time a request stop, Historic Monuments and Buildings Branch (as it was then called) took over the care and conservation of the station house and signal-box.

Green 1963, 80 and pl. 32; McCutcheon 1980, 107 and pl. 26.3; DOENI guide-card 1991

County Armagh

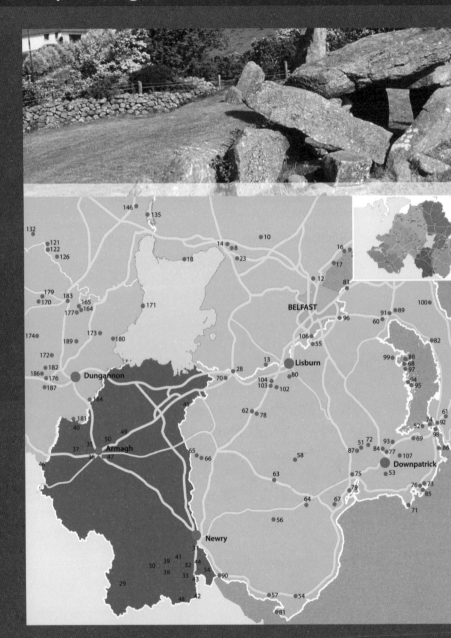

PREHISTORIC MONUMENTS

29. Annaghmare Cairn (H905178)
30. Ballykeel Dolmen and Cairn (H995213)
31. Ballymacdermot Cairn (J066240)
32. Clonlum North Cairn (J045214)
33. Clonlum South Cairn (J046206)
34. Clontygora Cairn (J098194)
35. Haughey's Fort (H835453)
36. The King's Stables (H839455)
37. Navan Fort (H847452 and area
38. Slieve Gullion South Cairn (J025203)
39. Slieve Gullion North Cairn (J021211)

EARLY CHRISTIAN PERIOD MONUMENTS

40. Eglish Crosses (H806502)
41. Killevy Churches (J040220)

42. Kilnasaggart Pillar Stone (J062149)
43. Lisbanemore Cashel (J078201)
44. Lisdoo Cashel (J081210)
45. Lisnamintry Rath (J046544)
46. Tynan Village Cross (H766430)

MEDIEVAL MONUMENTS

47. Armagh Friary (H876447)
48. Moyry Castle (J057146)

LATER MONUMENTS

49. Castledillon Obelisk (H909494)
50. North Meridian Markers (H878479)

County Armagh
Prehistoric Monuments

29 Annaghmare Cairn (H905178)

Location: 1³/₄ miles (2.8km) north of Crossmaglen in rough, boggy country. Park on the road and approach on foot through the forestry plantation. This is a court tomb, known locally as the Black Castle, and one of the finest examples in the north. The trapezoidal cairn encloses a three-chambered burial gallery, approached from the south through a

Annaghmare Cairn

horseshoe-shaped forecourt. The fine drystone walling is especially clear in the court. Excavation in 1962–1963 showed that the cairn had been extended northwards when two further chambers were added, approached from the cairn's long sides. The rough north end suggested to the excavator that a further extension was planned but never accomplished. Gabriel Cooney believes that the tomb was built at a significant site in the landscape, on a rocky knoll and over two hollows in the rock. Pottery sherds were found in the hollow under the third chamber, and there was a small standing stone in the court. Burned and unburned bone, flints and Neolithic pottery were found during the excavation.

D.M. Waterman in *Ulster J. Archaeol.* 28 (1965), 3–46; Herity 1987, esp. 179–181 and fig. 21; Cooney 2000, 93–94

30 Ballykeel Dolmen and Cairn (H995213)

Ballykeel Dolmen and Cairn

Location: 4¹/₂ miles (7.2km) south-west of Camlough at the west foot of Slieve Gullion, locally known as 'the Hag's Chair'. This impressive portal tomb (or tripod dolmen) is one of an important group of Neolithic stone monuments around Slieve Gullion. It stands at the south end of a long cairn, now 0.6–0.9m high, with a stone cist (not now visible) near the north end. The cairn was not a haphazard dump of stones; within it were two lines of stones, carefully set, parallel to the edges of the cairn. The dolmen is formed of two tall portal stones, with a high sill between, and a lower backstone, supporting a huge capstone, reinstated from a slipped position after excavation in 1963. Bone did not survive but there were plentiful finds of Neolithic pottery, including some fine decorated bowls.

A.E.P. Collins in *Ulster J. Archaeol.* 28 (1965), 47–70; Brett 1999, 3

31 Ballymacdermot Cairn (J066240)

Ballymacdermot Cairn

Location: 2 miles (3.2km) south-west of Newry, near Bernish viewpoint. This court tomb is set on the south slopes of Ballymacdermot Mountain, with magnificent views over the Meigh plain to Slieve Gullion and the ring-dyke mountains. The long, trapezoidal cairn had an almost enclosed circular forecourt at its north (uphill) end, its outline apparently influenced by the granite outcrop north-east of the court. Excavation in 1962 showed that original stone packing survived in the court and an antechamber. Beyond were two chambers, but no bone was found. Parts of the corbelled roofs of these chambers can still be seen. The cairn was first excavated in the early 19th century, and in 1962 the structure was further excavated and Neolithic pottery and flints were found. When the tomb was conserved for display, the low stone at the entry to the antechamber from the forecourt was added to facilitate drainage as no original sill was found.

A.E.P. Collins and B.C.S. Wilson in *Ulster J. Archaeol.* 27 (1964), 3–22; Herity 1987, esp. 181–183 and fig. 22

County Armagh
Prehistoric Monuments

32 Clonlum North Cairn (J045214)

Location 4 miles (6.4km) south-west of Newry, east of the foot of Slieve Gullion. These are the remains of a court tomb, badly damaged in the early 19th century when stone was reputedly removed for building Killevy Castle nearby. The court is of three-quarter enclosed form with an unusual small chamber in the west side. The burial gallery lacks subdividing stones but its length suggests there were originally three or four chambers. Not excavated.

Clonlum North Cairn

J. Bell in *Newry Magazine* 2 (1816), 235; *PSAMNI* 1940, 78

33 Clonlum South Cairn (J046206)

Location: 4½ miles (7.2km) south-west of Newry, 200yds (0.5km) east of Killevy Castle, in a field on the east side of a minor road. A roughly circular cairn, partly encroached on by cultivation, encloses a single rectangular chamber built of large slabs with a huge, now broken, capstone. Excavation in 1934 showed that the site was already

Clonlum South Cairn

thoroughly disturbed and produced few finds. This is likely to be a Neolithic portal tomb, but because of the damage that has occurred here it is now difficult to classify.

O. Davies and E.E. Evans in *Co. Louth Archaeol. J.* 8 (1934), 164–168; Ó Nualláin 1983, 81 and 90

34 Clontygora Cairn (J098194)

Location: 4 miles (6.4km) south of Newry within the south-east area of the Slieve Gullion ring-dyke, approached from a by-road east off the A1. This court tomb, locally known as the King's Ring, is badly damaged – some of its stones are said to have been used to build the Newry Canal – but it is still very impressive. The U-shaped forecourt, defined by tall stones, led into a gallery of probably three chambers. The chambers are built of very large stones with some roofing slabs still in position, but little cairn material survives.

Clontygora Cairn

Excavation in 1937 disentangled the monument from later field walls and found cremated bone, flints, Neolithic pottery, and Bronze Age pottery in a secondary context.

O. Davies and T.G.F. Paterson in *Proc. Belfast Nat. Hist. Phil. Soc.* 1 part 2 (1938), 20–42; Herity 1987, esp. 183–186 and figs 23–24

35 Haughey's Fort (H835453)

Location: West of the King's Stables (see below) and Tray Bog, the water source for both monuments. The hillfort is about 350m in diameter, contained originally by three banks and ditches. Excavation of the interior and part of the ditches showed that the fort was Bronze Age, active from about 1170 to 770 BC at the same time as Navan and King's Stables were in use. The high quality tools and weapons from the site reinforce the impression of a military society as described in the legends. Among the animal bones found (which included the remains of cattle and pigs) were the bones of the largest known dogs of this period in Ireland. The only visible feature is an oval field bank which roughly reflects the innermost circuit. No public access is available at present. The best view is from the King's Stables with Tray Bog in between.

County Armagh
Prehistoric Monuments

---

36 The King's Stables (H839455)

Location: 2¼ miles (3.6km) west of Armagh and about ⅝ mile (1km) north-west of Navan Fort, in Tray townland, reached by a turning north off Navan Fort Road (first right after Fort), along a winding lane to a lay-by and the path to the site. To the west Haughey's Fort is in clear view. The tree-grown bank of King's Stables is not a full circle; there is a break to the west. It encloses a circular pool, its surface largely covered with a mat of floating vegetation. Excavation in 1975 showed that the pool was man-made, about 25m across and 3–4m deep, with steeply sloping sides fed from a nearby stream through Tray Bog. It is partly filled with clay, mud and peat deposits, but originally it would have held clear water and there is still water under the surface vegetation. On the bottom of the pool

The King's Stables

were many animal bones with a surprising quantity of deer antlers and dog bones. Other finds included pieces of clay moulds for casting bronze swords and the facial part of a human skull. The finds and radiocarbon dates indicate the Late Bronze Age, (c. 1000–500 BC) and a ritual use is likely. This tree-grown pool is a place of strong atmosphere and it is not surprising that it has attracted stories, of a fierce dragon guarding its depths, and of its use to water the King of Ulster's horses, hence its name. On the other side of Navan Fort, in Loughnashade, a natural lake, the finest trumpet ever found in Ireland was amongst four discovered in the 19th century.

WARNING: The mat of vegetation on the surface of the pool is unstable. Do not try to access the pool itself, and keep children and animals away from the pool.

C.J. Lynn in *Ulster J. Archaeol.* 40 (1977), 42–62; *PoP* 1988, 19–21

37 Navan Fort (H847452 and area)

Location: 2 miles (3.2km) west of Armagh, north of the A28 to Killylea. The Navan Centre on the A28 is well signposted, has a large car park and a path leads north to the monument. Access can also be gained by turning off the A28 to Navan Fort Road and

Navan Fort Aerial View

there is a lay-by at the monument. Site identified as *Emain Macha*, chief residence of the kings of Ulster and prominent in heroic literature and legend, traditionally destroyed in AD 332. A huge, almost circular enclosure of over 12 acres occupies the summit of a low glacial hill which commands extensive views. Its ditch is inside the bank (so not defensive) and the enclosure is most impressive on its south and west sides.

In the north-west part of the interior is a tall mound, reconstituted after excavation in the 1960s and early 1970s. The earliest finds were Neolithic but the main activity was later. In the Late Bronze Age a circular enclosure was defined by a ditch with a ring of posts inside. Later, in the second century BC, in the Early Iron Age, a series of circular structures was built in this area. They had attached 'yards', all built in timber, and they were rebuilt many times, representing a long period of use. The finds, especially the skull of a Barbary ape from North Africa, point to high status involvement. The

County Armagh
Prehistoric Monuments

Navan Fort

enclosures were replaced by a massive structure, 40m in diameter, built of concentric rings of large posts round a massive central post dated by its tree rings to 95–94 BC. This structure was later filled with stones and burned, and a mound of sods and clay was built over the stone cairn to an overall height of about 5m.

A low circular enclosure near the centre of the fort was also partly excavated, and may be an Iron Age ring-barrow. Excavation in 1998 on the enclosing earthworks indicated that they are Iron Age in date, of the same period as the 40m structure, and further excavation in the interior has shown that there are other circular structures, similar to those under the high mound. Non invasive surveys of the monument show that there are many more features to be recovered in future. Limestone quarrying has approached very close to the east side of the site and has largely filled in Loughnashade, find-spot of the famous decorated Iron Age trumpet. The Navan Centre tells the story of Navan and the whole Navan landscape, and a visit is recommended. See also King's Stables (**36**) and Haughey's Fort (**35**).

Waterman 1997; Donnelly 1997, 38–43; DOENI guide book 1998; see also the journal *Emania* for news of continuing research

38 Slieve Gullion South Cairn (J025203)

Location: On the higher (south) summit of Slieve Gullion, approached along a signposted path adjacent to a car park, from the forest drive on the west. At 1894 feet (577m) this is the highest surviving passage tomb in the British Isles. It is known locally as 'Calliagh Berra's House'. It is dramatically sited and is visible from far away. For the visitor today access is difficult but the views are spectacular. A circular cairn with a revetment of large stones encloses an octagonal chamber, reached from the south-west along a short passage with sides of drystone-walling rather than large slabs. The passage is roofed with lintels, the chamber with corbelled stones, now partly collapsed. Excavation in 1961 showed that the burial deposits were badly disturbed, but there were fragments of cremated bone and flints. The 'bulge' on the cairn's north side results from the addition of a small round cairn, perhaps in the Bronze Age, but excavation produced no finds.

Slieve Gullion South Cairn

A.E.P. Collins and B.C.S. Wilson in *Ulster J. Archaeol.* 26 (1963), 19–40; A.G. Smith and J.R. Pilcher in *Ulster J. Archaeol.* 35 (1972), 17–21; V.A. Hall in *Proc. Roy. Irish Acad.* 90C (1990), 123–134

39 Slieve Gullion North Cairn (J021211)

Location: At the north end of Slieve Gullion summit ridge, at about 1,750 feet, approached by the same routes as the South Cairn, along the mountain and past the lake. This is a round cairn without kerb stones. Excavation in 1961 revealed two small cists, one with fragments of food vessel pottery and burned bone, suggesting an earlier Bronze Age date.

Slieve Gullion North Cairn

References as for South Cairn (**38**) above.

County Armagh
Early Christian Period Monuments

40 Eglish Crosses (H806502)

Location: 5¼ miles (8.5km) north-west of Armagh and 1½ miles (2.3km) west-south-west of Benburb, approached from Armagh on the B115, by a right turn to Benburb after the Drumsallan crossroads, or from Benburb south on the Carrickaness Road. A lane leads to the large, oval, hilltop graveyard. The name Eglish, from the Irish *An Eaglais*, 'the church', usually indicates a medieval parish church site, but here the crosses point to earlier use of the hilltop. The ruined structure nearby, not in state care, is what is left of a 1720 church, replaced by the present Drumsallan Church of Ireland church in 1821–1822.

Eglish Crosses

The North Cross has an ancient base and head but the shaft is new and the head is repaired. For many years the head was set directly in the base, but after it was knocked over and damaged in the 1970s the crosses were placed in state care in 1989 and this cross was repaired and restored. The head has an unpierced ring and decoration in a circular frame at the crossing on both faces: bossed spirals to the south and fine all-over interlace to the north.

The South Cross is part only of a head of the same form, but there is evidence that it originally had a finial. On each face is a deep hollow at or near the crossing, but this is probably not original decoration. This fragment was mounted on a stone plinth for its future safety. These two crosses share features with others in the Blackwater valley area and probably date from the late 9th or 10th century. Although battered and incomplete, they are reminders of what must have been an important early church here.

W. Reeves in *J. Roy. Soc. Antiq. Ireland* 16 (1883–1884), 425–426; Hamlin 1995, 187–196

41 Killevy Churches (J040220)

Killevy Churches

Location: 3 miles (4.8km) south of Camlough and 3½ miles (5.6km) south-west of Newry, on the lower east slopes of Slieve Gullion in Ballintemple townland. This is the site of one of Ireland's most important early convents, founded perhaps in the later 5th century by St Moninne (also called Darerca, daughter of Erc, or locally Bline). It was plundered by Vikings from Carlingford Lough in 923. Monastic life continued in the Middle Ages, when Killevy was a convent of Augustinian nuns until its suppression in 1542. A large granite slab in the north part of the graveyard traditionally marks St Moninne's burial. A round tower near the south-west corner of the church is known to have fallen in the 18th century but no trace survives.

The two churches are aligned in a row east-west and are linked by later walling, giving the impression of a single very long building. The west church is the older. Its west wall with the fine, massive lintelled door may date from the 10th or 11th century and it is the county's only surviving pre-Norman church. The rest of the church must date from the 12th century. The east church is medieval, from the time of the Augustinian convent. Its main feature is a decorated 15th-century east window. A stone with two carved crosses leaning against the west church's east wall (exterior) is an early grave-marker. A souterrain (not accessible) runs close to the graveyard, partly under the road. To the south-west, higher up the mountain, is St Bline's holy well, reached by a path which begins along the north side of the graveyard.

O. Davies in *Co. Louth Archaeol. J.* 9 no. 2 (1938), 77–86; Gwynn and Hadcock 1970, 321; Brett 1999, 16

County Armagh
Early Christian Period Monuments

---

42 Kilnasaggart Pillar Stone (J062149)

Location; 1¼ miles (2km) south of Jonesborough, close to the Louth border in Edenappa townland. Park at the road and approach through fields. A tall granite pillar marks the site of an early cemetery on one of Early Christian Ireland's great 'main roads', the *Slige Midlúachra*, running from Drogheda north through the Moyry Pass to Dunseverick in north Antrim. The long Irish inscription on the pillar's south-east face records the dedication of the place by Ternohc son of Ceran Bic under the patronage of Peter the Apostle. Ternohc's death is recorded in the annals at 714 or 716 and the pillar can be

Kilnasaggart Pillar Stone

Kilnasaggart Pillar Stone

dated to about 700. There are also three crosses on the south-east face and 10 on the north-west. Excavation in 1966 and 1968 uncovered an Early Christian cemetery with both stone-built and dug graves near the pillar, orientated east-west (not radially, as earlier claimed). Several small cross-carved slabs around the pillar may have served as grave-markers. The site was unenclosed in the mid 19th century; the present enclosure dates from early in the 20th century. A fine bullaun stone can be seen in the field to the west.

W. Reeves in *Ulster J. Archaeol.* 1 (1853), 221–225; an account of the excavation will appear in the forthcoming publication *An Archaeological Survey of County Armagh*

43 Lisbanemore Cashel (J078201)

Location: 4 miles (6.4km) south of Newry, close to (east of) the A1 road, in Killeen townland. A large cashel, diameter about 55m, has a ruined wall 3–4.5m thick at its base, partly removed on the south side. This was a farmstead enclosure of the Early Christian period, though no structures survive in the interior above ground. No secure access.

44 Lisdoo Cashel (J081210)

Location: In Killeen townland, 1km north of Lisbanemore. A similar but rather smaller enclosure. The oval cashel, measures about 34.5m by 39m, and has a surrounding wall, partly well preserved but damaged and rebuilt on its north side. A souterrain is reported in this cashel but it is not visible. No secure access.

45 Lisnamintry Rath (J046544

Location: 2 miles (3.2km) east of Portadown and 3 miles (4.8km) south-west of Lurgan, near Bluestone, approached from the road to the north-east (Ballygargan Road) by a signposted path. This once substantial rath has a circular central area with a perimeter bank, surrounded by a wide ditch, and there are remains of an outer bank and ditch. A gap to the north probably marks the entrance. This rath, with its mature trees, for a long time formed an attractive 'island' in farmland, but it is now surrounded by housing.

Brett 1999, 14

Lisnamintry Rath

County Armagh
Early Christian Period Monuments

46 Tynan Village Cross (H766430)

Location: At the road junction west of Tynan parish church. On or near the site of the hilltop parish church was an Early Christian church associated with St Vindic. Little is known of its early history but two stone crosses survive, the Village Cross and the Terrace Cross now at Tynan Abbey (not in state care), as well as a fragment in the graveyard and two pieces built into the graveyard wall (cross-base and ring fragment). The Village Cross is not in its original position, having been moved at least twice. It is composite, made up of two different crosses, the base and lower shaft of one being matched with the upper shaft and head of another. The lower shaft on the east side has a rectangular panel with Adam and Eve, and on the west side is another panel with a large figure and smaller figures behind. The head is mended and partly reconstructed,

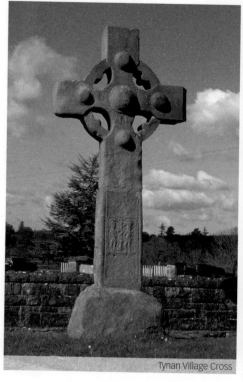

Tynan Village Cross

of open ringed form, decorated with tall bosses with traces of interlace. The shaft has panels of interlaced decoration. This cross, like the Eglish crosses, belongs to the Blackwater valley group and may date from the 10th century. On the nearby graveyard gatepost is an unusual hollowed stone, a 17th-century sundial, of which another example can be seen in Monaghan town.

W. Reeves in *J. Roy. Soc. Antiq. Ireland* 16 (1883–1884), 412–430; H. Roe in *Seanchas Ardmhacha* 1 no. 2 (1955), 112–113; Hamlin 1995, 187–196; Brett 1999, 10–11

County Armagh
Medieval Monuments

47 Armagh Friary (H876447)

Location: At the south-east edge of Armagh, reached by the drive off the ring-road which leads to the District Council offices (former archbishop's palace). Remains of the Franciscan friary church, founded by Dominican Archbishop Patrick Ó Scannail in 1263–1264. It had prominent patrons and played an important part in the city's religious life until it was suppressed in 1542. Some religious activity continued, but the buildings were involved in warfare later in the 16th century and were ruined by 1600. Since then they have been robbed for stone and incorporated in the landscaped demesne. The surviving remains are largely of the 13th-century church, 49.8m long (the longest known friary church in Ireland). The west end survives to a good height with a west door, and two of the original four arches (one

Armagh Friary

partly reconstructed), which open south into a missing aisle. Further east the church is more ruined, perhaps as a result of the fall of the tower, added in the 15th century at the junction of nave and chancel. Excavation in 1970 found no evidence for a south transept, which would usually be expected in such a long friary church. Two empty graves and two tomb recesses near the east end are reminders of the important patrons buried in the church, including Gormlaith O'Donnell, wife of Domhnall O'Neill, who died in 1353. The cloister north of the church has almost entirely disappeared but excavation in the 1960s showed foundations of buildings and traces of medieval occupation further north, near the ring-road.

Gwynn and Hadcock 1970, 242; C.J. Lynn in *Ulster J. Archaeol.* 38 (1975), 61–80; Brett 1999, 17

County Armagh
Medieval Monuments

48 Moyry Castle (J057146

Location: 7½ miles (12km) south-south-west of Newry, in Carrickbroad townland, close to Kilnasaggart (42), approached uphill under the railway bridge to west, and along a short path. The castle is set on a rocky height, overlooking the strategically important Moyry Pass *(Bealach an Mhaighre)*, the Gap of the North. The small tower, three stories high,

Moyry Castle

has rounded corners, gun-loops and a machicolation over the door. The two upper floors have fireplaces and windows, but the accommodation is unlikely to have ever been very comfortable. Fragmentary remains of the bawn wall survive. The castle was built in 1601 to secure the pass during Mountjoy's northern campaign, but it had a short military life.

Hayes-McCoy 1964, 2; Donnelly 1997, 107–108

County Armagh
Later Monuments

49 Castledillon Obelisk (H909494)

Location: On the summit of Cannon Hill, in Turcarra townland, reached by a minor road north off the A3, then an uphill walk. Difficult parking and best viewed from a distance. Castle Dillon, former home of the Molyneux family, is to the south-east. Tall, tapering shaft, a prominent landmark, with an inscription recording its erection in 1782 by Sir Capel Molyneux 'to commemorate the glorious revolution, which took place in favour of the constitution of the Kingdom, under the auspices of the volunteers of Ireland'.

Brett 1999, 266

50 North Meridian Markers (H878479)

North Meridian Markers

Location: On a hilltop in Tullyard townland, with extensive views, in a fenced enclosure in farmland, approached uphill from the adjoining road (off the Loughgall road), 1½ miles (2.4km) north of Armagh. These two prominent structures are unexpected in such a rural setting, but they are explained by the famous Armagh Observatory nearby. A stone arch with two pinnacles was built in the early 1790s, and a cast-iron obelisk on a stone base was added in 1864. These Northern Markers, together with a Southern Marker in the form of a pillar in Ballyheridan townland (a scheduled monument), provided stable reference points on the horizon for checking instruments in the Observatory, and various small features – a copper disc with a hole in the pinnacles, and a pointer in the top of the obelisk – allowed for fine adjustments and measurements. The arch is probably the work of Francis Johnston and the obelisk was made by the Gardner foundry in Armagh. These, together with the Southern Marker, are the only known surviving examples of this type of structure in Ireland. Castledillon Obelisk (**49**) is clearly visible on Cannon Hill to the east-north-east.

Butler 1992, 24–26; Brett 1999, 265

PREHISTORIC MONUMENTS

51. Annadorn Dolmen (J429459)
52. Audleystown Cairn (J562504)
53. Ballynoe 'Stone Circle' (J481404)
54. Dunnaman Court Tomb (J289151)
55. Giant's Ring (J327677)
56. Goward Dolmen (J244310)
57. Kilfeaghan Dolmen (J232154)
58. Legananny Dolmen (J288434)
59. Millin Bay Cairn (J629495)
60. Scrabo Hillfort (J477726)

EARLY CHRISTIAN PERIOD MONUMENTS

61. Derry Churches (J612524)
62. Dromore Cross (J200533)
63. Drumadonnell Cross
64. Drumena Cashel and Souterrain (J311340)
65. Lisnagade Fort (J086440)
66. Lisnavaragh Fort (J081442)
67. Maghera Church and Round Tower (J372342)
68. Nendrum Ecclesiastical Site (J524636)
69. Raholp Church (J540479)
70. Rough Fort (J142604
71. St John's Point Church (J527338)
72. Woodgrange Rath and Tower-House (J444465)

MEDIEVAL MONUMENTS

73. Ardtole Church (J564382)
74. Audley's Castle (J578506)
75. Clough Castle (J409403)
76. Cowd Castle, Ardglass (J561371)
77. Downpatrick, the Mound of Down (J483450)

78. Dromore Mound (J206532)
79. Dundrum Castle (J404370)
80. Duneight Motte and Bailey (J278608)
81. Greencastle (J247118)
82. Grey Abbey (J583681)
83. Holywood Motte (J401792)
84. Inch Abbey (J477455)
85. Jordan's Castle, Ardglass (J560371)
86. Kilclief Castle (J597457)
87. Loughinisland Churches (J423454)
88. Mahee Castle (J524639)
89. Movilla Abbey (J504744)
90. Narrow Water Castle (J127193)
91. Newtownards Priory (J493738)
92. Portaferry Castle (J593509)
93. Quoile Castle (J496470)
94. Ringhaddy Castle (J538588)
95. Ringhaddy Church (538590)
96. Shandon Park Mound (J385728)
97. Sketrick Castle (J525625)
98. Strangford Castle (J589498)
99. Tullynakill Church (J502645)

PLANTATION PERIOD AND LATER MONUMENTS

100. Ballycopeland Windmill (J579761)
101. Grey Point Fort (J457832)
102. Hillsborough Fort (J245586)
103. Hillsborough Courthouse (Market House) (J243586)
104. Hillsborough: Richhill Gates (J243586)
105. Kirkistown Castle (J645580)
106. Shaw's Bridge (J325690)
107. Struell Bath Houses and Wells (J513442)
108. The White House, Ballyspurge (J643550)

County Down
Prehistoric Monuments

51 Annadorn Dolmen (J429459)

Annadorn Dolmen

Location: 5¹/₂ miles (8.8km) south-east of Ballynahinch, on the north-east shore of Loughinisland Lake, within sight of Loughinisland Churches (**87**). A slightly displaced capstone covers a rectangular chamber of which three side stones survive. An early account suggests that this was formerly set in a large circular cairn and approached by a lintelled passage, so it may be the remains of a passage tomb. It is famous as the platform from which Thomas Russell addressed a crowd of United Irishmen in 1803, after the main 1798 rising. He was later hanged outside Downpatrick jail.

ASCD 1966, 78; DOENI leaflet 1998

52 Audleystown Cairn (J562504)

Audleystown Cairn

Location: Near the south shore of Strangford Lough, north-west of Castleward, approached from a turning off the A25 and across fields. Dual court tomb, discovered in 1946 and excavated in 1952. The trapezoidal long cairn, its sides revetted with neat drystone walling (partly restored), has a shallow forecourt at each end opening into four-chambered galleries. Traces of the corbelled stone roof were found. Excavation uncovered burial deposits in most, but not all, of the chambers, including burned and unburned human bones, animal bones, pottery sherds and flint implements. The human remains represented about 34 individuals, male and female adults and children.

A.E.P. Collins in *Ulster J. Archaeol.* 17 (1954), 7–56 and 22 (1959), 21–27; Herity 1987, esp. 200–205 and figs 32–33; Mallory and McNeill 1991, 60–61

53 Ballynoe 'Stone Circle' (J481404)

Location: 2¹/₂ miles (4km) south of Downpatrick, reached by a long footpath west off the minor road south from Downpatrick to Rathmullan, near the disused railway station. This large, complex monument was partly excavated in 1937–1939 but its development and date are still not entirely clear. The site appears now as a large circle of closely spaced stones

Ballynoe 'Stone Circle'

surrounding an oval mound, and some outlying stones. The east part of the mound has a stone kerb and there is an arc of stones beyond its west end. Excavation uncovered a slab feature with three compartments at the west end of the cairn, which could suggest the court tomb tradition, and a single stone cist at the east end which could point to the passage tomb tradition, but there is no generally accepted interpretation. Cremated remains representing at least seven individuals and some Neolithic pottery were found. Parallels for the outer stone circle with sites in Cumbria have been suggested. The site as we see it today is probably the result of a long development, and a late Neolithic to earlier Bronze Age date-range is likely.

ASCD 1966, 87–89; W. Groenman-van Waateringe and J.J. Butler in *Palaeohistoria* 18 (1976), 73–110; Mallory and McNeill 1991, 71–73

54 Dunnaman Court Tomb (J289151)

Location: 1¹/₈ miles (1.5km) west-north-west of Kilkeel, approached on a footpath north from the A2 beside the parochial house at Massfort. This impressive, unusually long gallery is built of split granite, and surviving jamb stones suggest that there were originally four segments. No sign survives of court stones or a cairn.

ASCD 1966, 73–74

County Down
Prehistoric Monuments

55 Giant's Ring (J327677)

Location: ¾ mile (1.2km) south of Shaw's Bridge, off the Ballylesson road in Ballynahatty townland, on an elevated site in a loop in the River Lagan. Large car park at entrance. The circular enclosure is about 190m (over 600ft) in diameter, and its bank is 3.6m high and 18.2m wide, made of material dug from the interior. There are now five gaps in the bank. Just east of the centre is a chambered tomb of five uprights with a large capstone,

Giant's Ring

probably the remains of a passage tomb. The earthwork is a henge, a late Neolithic ceremonial or assembly site, and it is the largest known in Ireland. Research and excavation during the 1990s on the ridge to the north confirms that this whole area was an important Neolithic ceremonial landscape, in which the Giant's Ring was the focus.

A.E.P. Collins in *Ulster J. Archaeol.* 20 (1957), 44–50; ASCD 1966, 89–91; Hartwell 1998, 32–44; Cooney 2000, 169–173

Giant's Ring - megalithic tomb

56 Goward Dolmen (J244310)

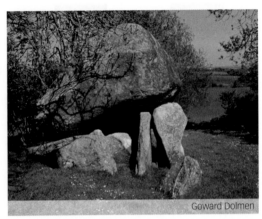

Goward Dolmen

Location: 2¹/₃ miles (3.7km) north-east of Hilltown, ¹/₄ mile (0.4km) south of the B8 Castlewellan to Hilltown road, on the north-west slopes of the Mourne Mountains. Lay-by at the monument. This fine portal tomb is surrounded by trees and is known locally as Pat Kearney's Big Stone, from the former owner (traces of his house are still visible). The enormous granite capstone has slipped from its original position over a rectangular chamber which faces north-east. Stones beyond the entrance suggest a curving façade, allied to the court tomb tradition. There has been no archaeological excavation, but there is an early report of the finding of an urn and a flint arrowhead.

ASCD 1966, 79–80; Ó Nualláin 1983, 81 and 95

57 Kilfeaghan Dolmen (J232154)

Kilfeaghan Dolmen

Location: 3⁷/₈ miles (6.2km) east-south-east of Rostrevor, reached by a lane north off the A2 coast road, just west of the Cassy Water, and a path across two fields. This portal tomb is at the north end of a long cairn, once much larger than is now visible, originally extending south downhill for 80–90ft (24.5–27.5m). The gigantic granite capstone is estimated to weigh some 35 tons and it may have been an erratic boulder already on the site, undermined and propped up with portal and side stones to form this spectacular dolmen. Excavation early in the 20th century discovered bone and pottery.

A.E.P. Collins in *Ulster J. Archaeol.* 22 (1959), 31–32; ASCD 1966, 80–81; Ó Nualláin 1983, 81 and 96

County Down
Prehistoric Monuments

58 Legananny Dolmen (J288434)

Location: 4 miles (6.4km) south of
Dromara and 5 miles (8km) north-west
of Castlewellan, at the side of a narrow
lane, on the south side of Cratlieve
Mountain in the Slieve Croob range,
with magnificent views of the Mourne
Mountains. This famous, much illustrated,
tripod portal tomb faces south and has
a large flat capstone gracefully balanced
on three unusually tall supporting

Legananny Dolmen

stones. Slight traces remain of a cairn, which must once have been far more extensive.
Nineteenth-century photographs show part of a court. There is an early record of 'urns'
having been found in the dolmen, but it has not been archaeologically excavated.

ASCD 1960, 81; Ó Nualláin 1983, 81 and 95; Donnelly 1997, 17–18

59 Millin Bay Cairn (J629495)

Location: 2¼ miles (3.6km) south-east of
Portaferry in Keentagh townland, close
to the east coast of the Ards peninsula
overlooking Millin Bay, approached along
a fenced path from the coast road. This
complex late Neolithic burial monument
appears now as an oval mound of
sand, grass-grown, with a surrounding
oval stone setting. Excavation in 1953
revealed a complicated sequence of
structures under the mound. Earliest was
a north-south stone wall, followed by
a long stone cist west of the wall, with
the bones of at least 15 individuals, neatly

Millin Bay Cairn

sorted and stacked. Around this and another small cist an oval of stone slabs was set,
externally supported by a bank of shingle, and the oval area was filled with shingle and
slabs. Outside the shingle bank seven more small cists were found, some with cremated
bone, and the whole area was finally covered with the long mound of sand in the outer
oval setting of stones. Many of the stones were decorated with pecked curvilinear and
rectilinear motifs, suggesting some possible link with the passage tomb tradition. Gabriel
Cooney points to the various ways in which human remains were treated: in the earlier

phase bones were carefully sorted and stacked, while later bodies were cremated and deposited in small, individual cists. Finds were sparse but a late Neolithic date is suggested.

Collins, Waterman and others 1955; *ASCD* 1966, 86–87; Cooney 2000, 121–124

60 Scrabo Hillfort (J477726)

Location: 30m from the main car park of Scrabo Country Park, south-west of Newtownards, the hillfort commands views over the whole of east Down. The 135ft (41m) tall 1857 tower, built in memory of the third Marquis of Londonderry, ensures that one can view the site from the sea and land for miles around. The earth bank enclosing an oval, 90m by 37m, was built with a stone core and had an inside ditch, now filled in. Although

Scrabo Hillfort

the earthwork is very degraded, its dramatic position demonstrates its original value as a look out and defence. Such forts are hard to date, but holes made when repairing the tower unearthed sherds of 'E' ware, roughly datable to 5th century AD. For comparison see also Mound of Down (77).

McErlean, McConkey and Forsythe, 2002

County Down
Early Christian Period Monuments

61 Derry Churches (J612524)

Location: 1¹/₂ miles (2.4km) north-east of Portaferry, east of the A2 to Cloghy, approached by a fenced path. Two small ruined churches stand on a rise in damp surroundings. There is written evidence of pre-Norman ecclesiastical activity on the site, associated with St Cumman, and there was a chapel here in 1302–1306. The south church is smaller and earlier, with *antae* to east and west, a west door and east and south windows. The stones were originally bonded with clay, not mortar, and there are cavities for scaffolding poles and horizontal intramural timbers in the walls. Some medieval alterations to the door and east window are marked by contrasting mortar. A 10th- or 11th-century date is likely, though a 12th-century one has also been suggested. The north church is larger, originally also built with clay, not mortar. It had a south door, an east window and perhaps a tower at the west end. A small early cross-carved stone is set in the north church. Excavation in 1962 showed Early Christian period occupation and a cemetery of stone-built graves under the churches, with an earlier building of stone and timber, perhaps a church, under the south church. Conservation following excavation included the straightening of the dangerously southward leaning north wall of the smaller church and the replacing of the original clay bonding material with similarly coloured mortar.

ASCD 1966, 290–291; D.M. Waterman in *Ulster J. Archaeol.* 30 (1967), 53–75

62 Dromore Cross (J200533)

Location: At the approach to the bridge over the River Lagan, at the edge of the cathedral graveyard. Park a little way away and walk back to the cross, taking care of passing traffic. The present cathedral must stand on or near the pre-Norman ecclesiastical site, associated with St Colmán, and the cross survives from this early activity. An inscription on the shaft records how it was re-erected in 1887, with much of the shaft and part of the head restored, after use elsewhere in the town as a market cross and the base of the town stocks. The head has an unperforated ring. Even in its fragmentary and weathered condition, it is possible to appreciate the impressive scale of the cross and the delicacy of the decorated panels on its shaft,

Dromore Cross

worked in the hard granite. It is difficult to date this cross, but the form and decoration suggest that a 9th-century date is possible. A cross-carved boulder, known as St Colmán's Pillow, also probably from the early church, is now kept in the cathedral chancel.

Atkinson 1925, 87–89; *ASCD* 1966, 274–275

63 Drumadonnell Cross

Location: Formerly built into the north gable of the school in Drumadonnell townland at J244392, but removed for safety when the school became derelict in the 1970s and re-erected, freestanding and under cover, in the Historic Monuments stone store in Castlewellan Forest Park (J335365). Accessible to visitors only by special arrangement. This impressive granite cross stands in a tall, cubical base. The head is ringed but unpierced, with a circular motif at the crossing on each face. Within the distinctive, wide edge mouldings are panels of interlaced and spiral decoration, badly weathered but still of great interest, which may date from the 9th century.

ASCD 1966, 301; Harbison 1990, 75–76 and figs 233–236

64 Drumena Cashel and Souterrain (J311340)

Drumena Cashel and Souterrain

Location: In the northern foothills of the Mournes, 2¼ miles (3.6km) south-west of Castlewellan, close to a minor road east-south-east off the A25 to Rathfriland, east of Lough Island Reavy. The oval cashel, has a wall 2.7–3.6m thick, partly rebuilt after excavation in 1925–1926. The gap to the east may be the original entrance rather than the narrow modern approach gap. Confused stones in the south part of the enclosure seem to be remains of house foundations. In the south-west area is a T-shaped souterrain (accessible), its walls of drystone construction and its roof lintelled (some lintels are replaced in concrete). The original entrance to the souterrain was by its south-east arm. Though not closely datable from excavated finds, this is a good example of a stone farmstead enclosure of the Early Christian period. There are other cashels in this rocky upland area.

ASCD 1966, 176–177; Donnelly 1997, 68–70

County Down
Early Christian Period Monuments

65 Lisnagade Fort (J086440)

Location: 3 miles (4.8km) south-west of Banbridge and 1¼ miles (2km) east-north-east of Scarva, approached across a field. This is one of Northern Ireland's most impressive earthworks, a rath with three massive banks and ditches (trivallate), partly planted with trees to form a landscape feature. In 1832 the ditches were apparently cleaned out, and in places they hold water in wet

Lisnagade Fort

weather. The original entrance to the south-east is marked by breaks in the banks and causeways over the ditches. Some excavation was done in 1950 but was not published. To the north, linked by banks and ditches, is a small circular rath excavated in 1953. This work showed that a square house was succeeded by a rectangular barn. The entrance was shown to be on the north side. Part of the line of the Dane's Cast linear earthwork runs close by, south of the fort.

ASCD 1966, 149–150 and 166

66 Lisnavaragh Fort (J081442)

Location: ³/₈ mile (0.6km) west of Lisnagade Fort, in Lisnagade townland, in the bend of a lane, with a modern house uncomfortably close to the fort. This impressive oval enclosure has three surrounding banks and two ditches (the outermost ditch is probably filled in). The original entrance through the substantial banks and ditches is from the south-east. An excavation carried out in 1951 revealed the stump of a massive gatepost at the entrance.

ASCD 1966, 150

67 Maghera Church and Round Tower (J372342)

Location: 2 miles (3.2km) north-north-west of Newcastle in Carnacavill townland, beside the Church of Ireland parish church. Gated drive from road leads to car park at church. The ruined round tower marks the site of an early church founded by the 6th-century St Domongart (Donard), after whom the highest peak in the Mourne Mountains is named. The tower stood to its full height until the early 18th century, when it fell in a great storm, and is now a stump 5.4m high. It is built of local granite boulders and shale and has the usual raised doorway, but this is a rough gap, without its dressings. Small-scale excavation in 1965 showed evidence of Early Christian activity near the tower. In the oval graveyard east of the parish church is the ruin of the medieval parish church, probably 13th century in date. It has a west door, unblocked during conservation work in the mid 1970s, and a small north window. A feature of the walls is voids left where horizontal intramural timbers have rotted away. At least two pre-Norman cross-carved stones survive in the graveyard and others are in store. Excavation before the graveyard extension south-west of the present church showed that the site is enclosed within a deep ditch, probably extending to form a large circular enclosure.

ASCD 1966, 306–307; Lalor 1999, 130–131

---

68 Nendrum Ecclesiastical Site (J524636)

Location: On Mahee Island, reached by twisting lanes and causeways off the A22 south of Comber. Car park at the site and small visitor centre displaying cross-carved stones from the site and other exhibits. This is the best example in Northern Ireland of a pre-Norman ecclesiastical enclosure with its buildings. Nendrum is associated with St Mochaoi who died at the end of the 5th century, and is linked with St Patrick in a much later source. Notices of Nendrum clergy, including three bishops, begin in the 7th century and the excavation of a sophisticated tide mill on the shore near the site has shown that

Nendrum Ecclesiastical Site

County Down
Early Christian Period Monuments

the mill was active in the early 7th century, which underlines the early importance of Nendrum. Annal references continue until a fire in 976, perhaps a Viking raid, when the head of the church (erenagh) was burned in his house. In the late 12th century a small Benedictine monastic cell was founded on the site, but by 1302–1306 this was the parish church, abandoned for Tullynakill on the mainland in the 15th century (see **99**).

Nendrum Sundial

H.C. Lawlor excavated the site from 1922 to 1924, when enclosure walls, church and round tower were restored. The glacial hill is crowned with three concentric walled enclosures, irregularly oval in plan. Little is known of the outer cashel, only partly in state care. In the middle cashel on the south-west side are circular platforms for huts, which excavation suggested were craft workshops, and a rectangular building known as the 'schoolhouse', also a workshop. In the inner cashel were the most important buildings, including the church with its graveyard and the base of a round tower north-west of the church. The west wall of the church was rebuilt in the 1920s, incorporating a reconstructed sundial at the south-west corner. Finds from the 1920s excavation, including the well-known bell of Nendrum, are in the Ulster Museum and Down Museum at Downpatrick. Underwater archaeological work in the 1990s showed that there is a stone jetty south-east of the enclosure, now inundated in the lough, and medieval pottery was found close by.

Lawlor 1925; *ASCD* 1966, 292–295; Gwynn and Hadcock 1970, 42, 107; DOENI guide-card (1997); Donnelly 1997, 56–59; Lalor 1999, 130–133; McErlean and Crothers, 2007; McErlean, McConkey and Forsythe, 2002

---

69 Raholp Church (J540479)

Location: 4 miles (6.4km) north-east of Downpatrick and about 2 miles (3.2km) north-east of Saul, off the Saul to Strangford road, approached across a field to a fenced area. This small pre-Norman church is associated with Bishop Tassach and is known locally as St Tassach's. Early sources tell us that Tassach administered the last sacraments to Patrick, but Tassach was at Raholp until much later. The church stands on a marked mound, in places revetted with drystone walling and large slabs. A simple rectangle, it has a west door with inclining jambs, and an east window with crosses incised on the straight lintel. An 11th-century date is possible. It continued in use in the Middle Ages and was listed as a parish church in the early 14th century. Doors were inserted in the north and south walls and the small north window was altered. The early masonry was bound with clay but the later work was mortared. By the 19th century the church was badly ruined and in about 1915 F.J. Bigger carried out extensive restoration work, including the present doorways and the stone altar. By the 1980s, when the site came into state care, it was

Raholp Church

again in a bad condition and in the 1990s a conservation programme was accompanied by excavation, when at least one burial was found underlying the south wall. A large slab east of the church with a socket must be a cross-base, and there were formerly many small cross-carved stones in the church but they have disappeared.

F.J. Bigger in *J. Roy. Soc. Antiq. Ireland* 46 (1916), 123–130; ASCD 1966, 295; R. Logue, C. Donnelly and R. McHugh in *Ulster J. Archaeol.* 62 (2003) 116–120

70 Rough Fort (J142604)

Location: 1/3 mile (0.5km) west of Moira at the roadside on Old Kilmore Road, in Risk townland. This is a well-preserved, unexcavated rath. The high, roughly circular central area is slightly dished, surrounded by a deep ditch, a bank and outer ditch, much silted up and partly occupied by the road. A causeway on the east side

Rough Fort

gives access to the central area. Although recent houses now surround the fort, we must thank the previous owner who, foreseeing the prospect of housing in this area, placed it in state care, so securing this important and attractive site.

Donnelly 1997, 64–67

County Down
Early Christian Period Monuments

Location: 1½ miles (2.4km) south-
south-west of Killough, near the
south-east tip of the Lecale peninsula
on the road to St John's Point
lighthouse. This small church, of the
10th or 11th century, marks the site of
an early establishment associated
with Eoan (John) son of Cairland, and
in medieval times it was a chapel.

St John's Point Church

It is an excellent example of a small,
pre-Romanesque church with a lintelled west door with sloping jambs, *antae* to east and
west and a south window. This stone church was almost certainly preceded by a wooden
church. Small-scale excavation in 1978 discovered burials under the north wall but no
sign of the claimed radial arrangement of graves around the church. At the roadside,
outside the enclosed area, is a holy well and an elongated hollowed stone, probably a
form of grinding stone.

ASCD 1966, 295; N.F. Brannon in *Ulster J. Archaeol.* 43 (1980), 59–64; *PoP* 1988, 29–30

72 Woodgrange Rath and Tower-House (J444465)

Location: 3½ miles (5.6km) south of Crossgar, 1 mile (1.6km) north-east of Annadorn
Dolmen (**51**). Platform rath on hilltop with the remains of a tower-house on its north-west
side. This is a stretch of wall 3.6m long with one splayed loop. Nothing is presently known
about its history. Another rath with an added tower-house can be seen (not in state care)
at Castleskreen (J466400) in the Lecale district.

ASCD 1966, 255

County Down
Medieval Monuments

73 Ardtole Church (J564382)

Ardtole Church

Location: ¾ mile (1.2km) north-north-east of Ardglass, east of the A2, on the A22, with a lay-by across the road from the site. The church stands on a prominent hilltop overlooking the sea and with views to the Isle of Man. An early cross slab from this site, now built into the church at Chapeltown, and a souterrain south of the church suggest Early Christian period activity on the hilltop. The ruin is of the medieval parish church, dedicated to St Nicholas, and there is a tradition that it was abandoned after a massacre. The long narrow church seems largely of 15th-century date, with a huge east window and opposed north and south doors, one with a draw-bar hole.

F.J. Bigger in *J. Roy. Soc. Antiq. Ireland* 46 (1916), 130–135; *ASCD* 1966, 298

74 Audley's Castle (J578506)

Audley's Castle

Location: 1 mile (1.6km) north-west of Strangford in Castleward townland, on a rocky height overlooking Strangford Lough, signposted from the Downpatrick to Strangford (A25) road. This 15th-century tower-house was built by the Audley family, but passed to the Wards in 1646 and was used in 1738 as an eye-catching focus of the long vista along Castle Ward's Temple Water. Though the bawn is ruined, its full circuit can be traced, running south to the cliff edge. The tower-house, like Kilclief (86), is of 'gatehouse' type with two projecting towers linked by a high arch (machicolation) to defend the entrance. In one tower were latrines and in the other a spiral stair leads to first and second floor rooms and the roof. The first floor room has a reconstructed wooden floor and semicircular stone barrel vault. The tower is well provided with domestic comforts, like cupboards, window-seats, latrines and drain holes for slops.

ASCD 1966, 225–227; Donnelly 1997, 100–102

County Down
Medieval Monuments

75 Clough Castle (J409403)

Clough Castle

Location: At the junction of the A25 and A24 in Clough village, in a strategically important site with commanding views. This is an excellent example of an Anglo-Norman earthwork castle with added stone tower. A small kidney-shaped bailey lies south of a large mound, originally separated from it by a 2.1m-deep ditch. Excavation on the mound's summit in 1950 revealed that originally (late 12th or very early 13th century) there was a timber palisade round the summit. Pits uncovered within the palisaded area have been interpreted as being used by archers. The foundation of a long rectangular hall was found in the north-east half of the area, probably built in the mid 13th century, and

Clough Castle

later in the century a small rectangular stone keep was built to the south-west. This still survives, two storeys high. In the late Middle Ages, apparently after a period of disuse, it was restored and added to, resulting in an L-shaped tower-house, though the precise phases of use of this site have been debated. Dudley Waterman's excavation at this site in 1950 was a pioneering piece of research.

D.M. Waterman in *Ulster J. Archaeol.* 17 (1954), 103–163; *ASCD* 1966, 200–203; McNeill 1997, 64 and 72

76 Cowd Castle, Ardglass (J561371)

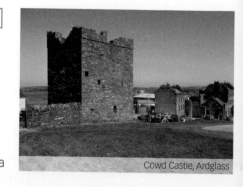

Cowd Castle, Ardglass

Location: At the entrance to Ardglass golf-club, overlooking the sea. Cowd Castle belongs to an important group of tower-houses in the medieval port of Ardglass. Downhill is the Ardglass Castle complex, incorporating an important medieval warehouse range, and uphill is Margaret's Castle, partly masked by a house. Cowd is a small squarish tower of the 15th or 16th century, viewable only from the outside. It is built of split stone rubble and has a battered base. Inside are two floors and an attic, with a wall-walk above, originally providing the only access to the tower. There are narrow loops on the ground floor and two windows with window-seats on the first floor. Originally this tower was linked to the town wall and access to the floors below was by stairs attached to the wall thickness. The door in the west wall at ground floor level was inserted later. It cuts through one of the stairs in the wall. See also Jordan's Castle (**85**).

ASCD 1966, 222; Mallory and McNeill 1991, 286–287

77 Downpatrick, the Mound of Down (J483450)

Location: On the north-west outskirts of Downpatrick, strongly sited on the edge of the Quoile marshes, approached by a path leading north from Mount Crescent. Known as the Mound of Down, Dundalethglas, English Mount and Rathkeltair, this is one of the major earthworks of Northern Ireland, consisting of an egg-shaped enclosure, defined by a steep bank and wide outer ditch. The original entrance is on the south side away from the marsh. In the south-east part of the interior is a high, U-shaped mound with its own surrounding ditch. The large earthwork is probably a pre-Norman enclosure, a royal

The Mound of Down

headquarters of the Dál Fiatach, reused as the site of an Anglo-Norman castle mound of the late 12th century, but the mound was either unfinished or later altered for artillery. The cathedral is built on a similarly fortified hill close by. The Mound of Down has not been archaeologically excavated, and there is much more to be learned from the study of this site.

Irish Naturalists Journal 6 (1936–1937), 118; *ASCD* 1966, 202–203; McNeill 1997, 12–13

County Down
Medieval Monuments

78 Dromore Mound (J206532)

Location: In Ballyricknacally townland on the east outskirts of Dromore, on the south side of Mount Street. The mound lies in a bend of the River Lagan, commanding the valley, with extensive views. This is the best-preserved and most impressive example in Ulster of an Anglo-Norman motte and bailey castle. The mound rises 12.2m high above its

Dromore Mound

encircling ditch, blocking the landward approach from the north. To the south is the small, squarish bailey above the river. An outer bank and ditch provide further protection to east, north and north-west. Excavation on the motte in 1951 showed that the first summit defence was a timber palisade, followed by the low bank which is still visible.

D.M. Waterman in *Ulster J. Archaeol.* 17 (1954), 164–168; *ASCD* 1966, 203–204

79 Dundrum Castle (J404370)

Location: On a wooded hill north-west of Dundrum village, with fine views over sea, mountains and inland. Large car park below the castle. Fortified in pre-Norman times (there is a souterrain in the adjoining field), this hilltop was chosen by John de Courcy in or soon after 1177 for one of his coastal castles, dominating Dundrum Bay and the

Dundrum Castle

access to Lecale. Captured by King John in 1210, the castle passed to the Earls of Ulster in 1227 but in the later Middle Ages was in Irish hands (the Magennises). The earliest stone castle was the polygonal upper ward on the highest part of the hill with surrounding rock-cut ditches. The marks of buildings attached to the wall can still be seen. The circular keep originally had a first floor entrance, and excavation revealed a rock-cut well. It was heightened in the 15th century.

Dundrum Castle

The twin-towered gatehouse was added later in the 13th century, approached by a narrow path up the rock and requiring a right angled turn by attackers, overlooked from the east tower. The polygonal lower ward was added in the 15th century by the Magennises. The latest building at the site is the house in the south-west corner, built by the Blundell family in the 17th century (possibly on the site of, or incorporating, an earlier structure), which was once a fine dwelling.

D.M. Waterman in *Ulster J. Archaeol.* 14 (1951), 15–29 and 27 (1964), 136–139; ASCD 1966, 207–211; Donnelly 1997, 84–86; McNeill 1997, 26–28, 53–54, 91–92 and 194–196

80 Duneight Motte and Bailey (J278608)

Duneight Motte and Bailey

Location: 2 miles (3.8km) south of Lisburn and ¹/₂ mile (0.8km) east of Ravernet. A fine Anglo-Norman motte and bailey, strategically sited on the north bank of the Ravernet River to command the valley route. The motte is triangular in plan, separated from the bailey by a ditch. The bailey is a truncated oval, protected by a ditch and bank and an extra ditch to the east, but on the river side (south) the defences are less formidable. Excavation in 1961 showed that the bailey was a remodelled pre-Norman enclosure. Parts of wooden and stone buildings were found in this enclosure and slighter structures outside to the east. It can probably be identified with *Dún Echdach*, royal fort of Dál Fiatach kings, mentioned in the annals in 1003 and in 1010, when a distinction was made between the *dún* (fort) and *baile* (perhaps the settlement outside). Excavation also uncovered a collared urn with a cremation burial, evidence of activity beside the river in the Bronze Age.

D.M. Waterman in *Ulster J. Archaeol.* 26 (1963), 55–78; ASCD 1966, 205–206; Donnelly 1997, 86–87

County Down
Medieval Monuments

Location: 4 miles (6.4km) south-west of Kilkeel, reached by minor roads off the A2 from Kilkeel or Lisnacree and down a drive to car park at the castle. Prominently sited on a rocky outcrop close to Greencastle Point, the castle commands the narrow entry to Carlingford Lough and is within sight of Carlingford Castle. A royal castle, built in about 1250, it had an eventful military history. Attacked and damaged by Brian O'Neill and Hugh O'Connor in 1260, besieged and taken by Edward Bruce in 1316, attacked and spoiled by the Irish at least twice in the later 14th century, it was still maintained as a garrison for Elizabeth I by Bagnall in the 1590s. Coastal patrols, contact with Dublin and the trade of produce from the area made the two castles an important strategic unit.

Greencastle

The castle is approached across an impressive rock-cut ditch, partly excavated and left open. The curtain wall with four corner towers enclosed a trapezoidal area but is badly ruined. The best-preserved stretch is visible in the farmyard on the south-west. The north-east tower was excavated and conserved and part of the east curtain, found collapsed intact into the ditch, was reconstructed near the car park. The narrow wall crossing the ditch was intended as a dam, but the rock would not hold the water. The large rectangular keep or hall is of the 13th century but with substantial 15th- and 16th-century alterations. It was originally entered by a first floor door on the south, protected by a forebuilding (excavated foundations visible). A ground floor door in the west wall is a 15th-century alteration and the rough gap near the south-east angle (the present entrance) is a late forced entry. The cross walls dividing the ground floor into three vaults are also 15th-century insertions. At first floor level was the great hall (late medieval windows and fireplace) with a latrine in the north-east corner. The upper parts of the hall,

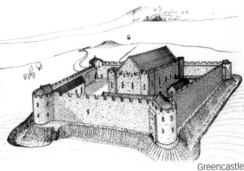

Greencastle

with mural passages, wall-walks and angle turrets, date from a 15th-century remodelling. Fragments of other buildings in the ward include part of a long rectangular structure south-west of the keep. A long series of excavations has been carried out here as part of the conservation programme.

A motte and a church ruin survive nearby.

D.M. Waterman and A.E.P. Collins in *Ulster J. Archaeol.* 15 (1952), 87–102; *ASCD* 1966, 211–219; C. Gaskell-Brown in *Ulster J. Archaeol.* 42 (1979), 51–65; PoP 1988, 66–69; McNeill 1997, 88–91 and 193

82 Grey Abbey (J583681)

Grey Abbey

Location: On the east edge of Greyabbey village, beside the Rosemount estate, with a car park at the entrance. There is a small visitor centre with displays at the entrance and a reconstructed 'medieval' physic (herb) garden. With Inch Abbey, Grey is the best example of Anglo-Norman Cistercian architecture in Ulster. It is the daughter-house of Holm Cultram (Cumbria), founded in 1193 by John de Courcy's wife, Affreca. Poor and decayed in the late Middle Ages, the abbey was dissolved in 1541, but in the early 17th century was granted to Sir Hugh Montgomery and the nave was refurbished for parish worship until the late 18th century. The remains, in the beautiful parkland setting of the nearby grand house of Rosemount, consist of the church with cloister and surrounding buildings to the south. The abbey was formerly very close to the shores of Strangford Lough, but the sea is now hidden from view at the abbey by the parkland of Rosemount. There is also a stream and a well within the parkland that are thought to have been used by the monks who once lived at Greyabbey.

The church, entered through an elaborate west door, has an aisleless nave, transepts with two chapels in each, and a short chancel lit by tall lancet windows. The buildings round the cloister include a once fine aisled chapter house and a still impressive refectory with beautiful windows, a reader's pulpit and a hatch to the kitchen. The west range and cloister walks have disappeared as at Inch. Possibly they were built of lighter materials. The three buttresses propping the south wall of the nave are part of a major conservation programme carried out early in the 20th century.

ASCD 1966, 275–279; Stalley 1987, 245 and elsewhere; DOENI guidebook (1990); McErlean, McConkey and Forsythe, 2002, 419–420

83 Holywood Motte (J401792)

Location: On the north side of Brook Street, in Ballykeel townland, originally overlooking Belfast Lough, but now in built-up surroundings. Anglo-Norman castle mound, formerly probably with a ditch round its base and a timber palisade round the summit, but now with a spiral path and planted with trees, the result of 19th-century landscaping. King John stayed at Holywood in 1210 and a castle at Holywood is mentioned in 1234, but it is not known whether either reference applies to this motte. A fine 13th-century church (the ruins now known as Holywood Friary) in the town was contemporary with the castle.

ASCD 1966, 194

84 Inch Abbey (J477455

Inch Abbey

Location: ³/₄ mile (1.2km) north-west of Downpatrick, reached via the Inch Abbey Road, just of the main A7. Site has a car park. This beautiful site, on the north bank of the Quoile, was originally an island in the Quoile Marshes. A pre-Norman church here, called *Inis Cumhscraigh*, was plundered by Vikings in 1002. Its large earthwork enclosure has been traced from air photos and partly survives. The visible remains are of the Cistercian abbey, daughter-house of Furness (Lancs), founded in the 1180s by John de Courcy in atonement for his destruction of Erenagh, 3 miles (4.8km) to the south. The Cistercian precinct was enclosed by a bank and ditch and is mostly in state care, extending north to south from the parish graveyard to the river and east to west up the valley sides. The buildings are mainly of the late 12th and 13th centuries. The church must be slightly later than the church at Grey Abbey. It had an aisled nave, transepts with pairs of chapels, and a chancel lighted, like Grey Abbey, by graceful grouped lancet windows. In the 15th century, when the monastic community was smaller, the church was altered by walling-in the chancel and first bay of the nave and blocking off the transepts; a much smaller church was created and the rest was abandoned. The cloister walks to the south have disappeared but foundations of the east and south ranges remain, on a more modest scale than at Grey Abbey, as well as outlying buildings towards the river. These include an infirmary, a possible guesthouse, and a bakehouse with a well nearby. Down Cathedral is clearly visible across the river.

ASCD 1966, 279–281; A. Hamlin in *Ulster J. Archaeol.* 40 (1977), 85–88; Stalley 1987, 246; Donnelly 1997, 88–91

85 Jordan's Castle, Ardglass (J560371)

Jordan's Castle

Location: In Ardglass, between Kildare Street and Quay Street, commanding the harbour. This late 15th-century tower-house is the largest of the impressive group which testifies to the importance of Ardglass as a town and port in the Middle Ages (see also Cowd (**76**)). The castle is named after Simon Jordan who withstood a long siege here in 1601. The characteristic projecting towers with a high machicolation arch face north, and the entrance is protected by a smaller machicolation at right angles to the main arch. The west tower contains a spiral stair and the east tower latrines at two levels. The ground floor chamber has a semicircular barrel vault with impressions of wicker centring. There are three chambers above, all with modern timber ceilings. The antiquarian Francis Joseph Bigger bought the castle in 1911 and restored it, fitting it out with furniture and bequeathing it to the state in 1926. The figure corbels on the third floor are modern copies of 14th-century figures in St Francis's Priory, Kilkenny. The present flat roof is also modern: originally the roof was gabled, with a pigeon-loft in one tower. Excavation in the castle grounds in the late 1990s suggested that a stone warehouse adjoined the tower-house.

ASCD 1966, 223–225; Mallory and McNeill 1991, 287

County Down
Medieval Monuments

86 Kilclief Castle (J597457)

Location: 2¹/₂ miles (4km) south of Strangford on the A2, facing the sea. Car park opposite. Impressive tower-house, reputedly built by John Sely, bishop of Down, between 1413 and 1441 when he was dismissed for living with Letticia Thomas, a married woman, in his castle at Kilclief. This makes it the earliest datable tower-house in Co. Down, and this monument is often used to date other tower-houses in the county. Its features include the high machicolation arch between projecting towers, a local feature displayed here, at Audley's Castle and at Margaret's and Jordan's Castles in Ardglass. The machicolation protects the entrance leading to a spiral stair in the south-east tower. In the north-east tower is a latrine shaft with access from three of the four floors. As at Jordan's Castle, the ground floor chamber has a semicircular barrel vault built on wicker centring. On the second floor a 13th-century coffin-lid from the nearby church was reused as a lintel for the fireplace and on the third floor crosses can be seen cut into a window. The two-light window in the east wall is a modern reconstruction based on a surviving fragment.

Kilclief Castle

ASCD 1966, 233–235

87 Loughinisland Churches (J423454)

Location: In Tievenadarragh townland, 4 miles (6.4km) west of Downpatrick and 1 mile (1.6km) east of the A24 Belfast to Newcastle road. Now reached by a causeway, this atmospheric graveyard was originally on an island in the lake. A remarkable group of three ruined churches stands in the large graveyard overlooking the lake. The earliest recorded reference is to a parish church here in 1302–1306. The Middle Church is the oldest, probably of the 13th century, with a draw-bar hole to secure the south door. The large North Church was built in the 15th century, probably to replace the Middle Church, and continued in use until 1720. Smallest and latest is the South (MacCartan's) Church. It had a two-light east

Loughinisland Churches

window with pointed heads, and the west door is carved with the date 1636 and the initials PMC for Phelim MacCartan. The MacCartans had one of their chief seats near the lake and this was probably their principal burial ground.

ASCD 1966, 305–306

88 Mahee Castle (J524639)

Mahee Castle

Location: Commanding the north end of Mahee Island in Strangford Lough, now reached by a causeway, but formerly by a ford. Visitors should park at Nendrum (**68**) and walk the short distance back to the castle. This tower-house, said to have been built in 1570 by an English soldier, Captain Browne, is badly ruined but is still of considerable interest. Rectangular and fairly small in ground plan, it was entered by a door in the north-west wall which has a draw-bar socket and a murder-hole. To the left of the door was a stair to the next floor. There are two ground floor rooms, the larger with a semicircular vault built on plank centring and the smaller with a pointed vault built on paired wicker mats. The smaller room, once thought to be a secure boat bay, may be just a storeroom (compare nearby Sketrick (**97**)). There were two storeys above, but the upper parts are ruined. Part of the bawn wall survives to the south-west, cut into the hill.

ASCD 1966, 244–245; McErlean, McConkey and Forsythe, 2002, 112–115

89 Movilla Abbey (J504744)

Movilla Abbey

Location: 1 mile (1.6km) east of Newtownards, on the side of the B172 to Millisle, approached from the south through the large cemetery. This hilltop was occupied by one of Ulster's most important early churches and scholarly centres, associated with the 6th-century St Finnian. Excavation prior to housing development north of the church showed that the early community was large and hard-working. Remains of thousands of pots, metal-working debris and glass work remains were found. Plundered by Vikings in 824, it was refounded in the 12th century as an abbey of Augustinian Canons dedicated to St Malachy, and survived until the suppression of religious houses in the 1540s. One stone only survives from the pre-Norman period: a slab with a sharply-cut ringed cross and an inscription asking for a prayer for Dertrend, *or do Dertrend*. The ruined church is long and narrow, its south wall largely lacking and north wall much rebuilt. It is partly 13th and partly 15th century in date. The altered east window has plain intersecting tracery, later blocked, incorporating an earlier, small, semicircular-headed window. In the west gable is a two-light transomed 15th century window with carved decoration. Built into the inside of the north wall is the best collection in the north of 13th-century coffin-lids with foliate crosses. Shears indicate a woman's burial and a sword a man's. The pre-Norman slab is at the west end of the row.

ASCD 1966, 283–284; Gwynn and Hadcock 1970, 188; M.J. Yates in *Ulster J. Archaeol.* 46 (1983), 53–66; R.J. Ivens in *Ulster J. Archaeol.* 47 (1984), 71–108; *PoP* 1988, 50–52; Mallory and McNeill 1991, 268; McErlean, McConkey and Forsythe, 2002, 77

---

90 Narrow Water Castle (J127193)

Location: 5 miles (8km) south-east of Newry beside the A2 to Warrenpoint, picturesquely and strategically sited on a promontory in the Newry River. Tower-house and bawn were built in the 1560s at a cost of £361 4s 2d for an English garrison, but later in that century it was in the hands of the Gaelic Magennis family. A lease of 1570 refers to 'nine cottages covered with earth within the precinct of the said castle'. The tower entrance in the west wall was protected by a forebuilding and a corbelled machicolation above, with a

Narrow Water Castle

murder-hole immediately inside. Gun-loops on the corner provided extra cover. There are chambers at three levels with an attic, and straight stairs, latrines and other small chambers in the wall thickness. The first floor room has a semicircular barrel vault built on wicker centring. The present roof and some windows are restorations of the 1960s, and wicker centring from that restoration has been left in position in two windows to demonstrate this characteristically Irish method of construction. There was a wall-walk behind the stepped battlements, commanding extensive views. The bawn wall has been modified by later use (the site was used for industrial purposes in the late 18th century) but it must represent the extent of the original enclosure, with part of the promontory to the west left for a small boat quay.

ASCD 1966, 241–243

91 Newtownards Priory (J493738)

Newtownards Priory

Location: At the south-east edge of the town. Its tower is a familiar landmark on Court Street. These are the only substantial remains in Northern Ireland of a Dominican (Black) Friary, founded in the mid 13th century. The lower parts of the nave are of the 13th century, with two blocked doors in the south wall leading to the now vanished cloister. Extensive 14th-century remodelling involved rebuilding the upper parts of the nave, extending it westwards and adding a north aisle reached through the surviving arcade. In the early 15th century the arcade became unstable and the repairs involved rebuilding the west wall and providing a new west door. The friary was suppressed in 1541 and burned in 1572, but after the Plantation it was granted to Hugh Montgomery, first Viscount Ards, who refurbished the church,

Newtownards Priory

rebuilding the north aisle and adding the tower. The door in the tower is elaborately decorated in a Renaissance style and bears his initials, HLM, but the soft Scrabo sandstone has weathered badly and much of the detail is now unclear. For this reason a copy of the door was made by Historic Monuments craftsmen and in 1607 was set in the modern wall, not far from its model. The church continued in use until a grand new one was built from 1817 onwards, and for some years in the early 19th century part of the church was used as a courthouse. In 1890 it was consecrated as the burial place of the Londonderry family. The cloister of the friary was adapted for Montgomery's use in the 17th century, when the Castle Gardens were laid out (now a scheduled historic monument). Walls and gate pillars from the 17th century survive at the Castle Gardens.

ASCD 1966, 284–287; Gwynn and Hadcock 1970, 228

92 Portaferry Castle (J593509)

Portaferry Castle

Location: Prominently sited on the slope overlooking Portaferry harbour, within sight of Strangford and Audley's Castles across the water, this is a 15th- or 16th-century tower-house, built by the Savage family. Simpler than the earlier 'gatehouse' type (see Audley's Castle (74)), it is square in plan with one projecting tower to the south. Here a small machicolation arch defends the door. There are three storeys and an attic, and the projecting tower rises higher than the rest of the building containing both stairs and latrines. Like early tower-houses it has spiral stairs, but like some later ones it lacks a stone vault, all the floors being originally of wood. The east angle is ruined and the castle is a shell, visible only from outside. The adjoining stable block is a Tourist Information Centre and is used for displays, sometimes featuring monuments.

ASCD 1966, 245–246; McErlean, McConkey and Forsythe, 2002, 213–214

93 Quoile Castle (J496470)

Quoile Castle

Location: 1½ miles (2.4km) north-north-east of Downpatrick, north of the A25, near the south bank of the Quoile River, beside the Quoile Countryside Centre. The river is navigable to Strangford Lough. These are the remains of a late 16th-century tower-house, inhabited into the 18th century. The south angle has fallen, revealing an interesting cross-section through vaults and floors. The entrance in the north-east wall was protected by a murder-hole. On the ground floor were two chambers, each stone-vaulted (showing marks of wicker centring), with many small gun-loops. A straight stair in the wall thickness led from the door to first floor level, and another to the second floor. Both floors had fireplaces. There is access to the ground and first floor levels.

ASCD 1966, 247–248

94 Ringhaddy Castle (J538588)

Location: 8 miles (12.8km) south-east of Comber and 2 miles (3.2km) south-east of Killinchy, approached on minor roads off the A22. At quay turn left through gate and along lane to castle on Castle Island. This is one of the most completely surviving tower-houses in the county, retaining its gables and formerly an original wooden window (now removed from the site and conserved in the NIEA Built Heritage headquarters building in Belfast). There were at least two main phases of construction at this site. The ground floor, which had a stone vault, dates from the 15th century, while the upper parts were rebuilt in about 1600. It is rectangular in plan with small turrets at the north-east and south-west angles, one with the stair and the other with a latrine chute. There are large fireplaces on the first and second floors, and an attic in the roof. A distinctive stone rainwater spout projects from the east side. The castle seems to have changed hands between Bryan McArt and the English in the early 16th century, and it is likely that the earlier castle was McArt's stronghold, slighted when he withdrew, and rebuilt by the new English owner. Underwater investigation has confirmed the presence of a stone slipway beside the castle, and water transport was clearly of great importance in this location. Ringhaddy Church (**95**) is on the hill beyond the castle.

ASCD 1966, 248–250; McErlean, McConkey and Forsythe, 2002, 102–111

95 Ringhaddy Church (538590)

Location: Beautifully sited on the prominent glacial hill, north of the castle (**94**), overlooking Strangford Lough. The ruined church stands inside a low circular earthwork enclosure, possibly the remains of a tree ring. The church is a simple rectangular ruin and all dressed stones are missing. There are opposed doors in the north and south walls, with draw-bar holes, windows in the east, north and south walls, and small cupboards near the east end. The local rubble stonework with small pinnings is best seen in the exterior west wall where scaffolding (putlog) holes are visible. A church, apparently parochial, was listed in the 1302–1306 taxation, but it is hard to date this ruin: it could be of the 13th or the 15th century.

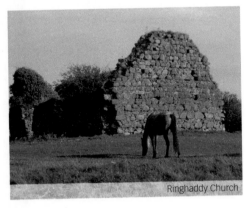

Ringhaddy Church

Reeves 1847, 9–10; *ASCD* 1966, 309; McErlean, McConkey and Forsythe, 2002, 102–103

County Down
Medieval Monuments

96 Shandon Park Mound (J385728)

Location: One of Belfast's few surviving medieval earthworks, reached by a path between numbers 45 and 47 Shandon Park in Knock. The mound, strategically sited on high ground with extensive views, is now conspicuous because planted with conifers. It is probably a motte, an Anglo-Norman castle mound, but the name *sean dún* (old fort) leaves open the possibility that this motte, like some others, was built on a pre-Norman fort site. Old Knock graveyard is on another hill *(an cnoc)* close by and it may also be an early site.

ASCD 1966, 194

97 Sketrick Castle (J525625)

Location: Island site off the west coast of Strangford Lough, now reached by a causeway, 5³/₄ miles (9.2km) south-east of Comber. A castle here is mentioned in written sources as involved in warfare in 1470, so a mid 15th-century date has been suggested, but the present large tower-house is probably later, perhaps built in the 16th century on earlier foundations. It was actively involved in 16th-century warfare but stood fairly complete until 1896, when about half collapsed in a storm. It was four storeys high. The door in the east wall was defended by a murder-hole. There were four chambers at ground floor level, the largest with a vault built on wicker centring and two ovens. The central space was a boat bay or storeroom, as at Mahee Castle (**88**), and the small, unlighted room could have been a lock-up or a treasury. The upper floors are

Sketrick Castle

badly ruined but the joist-holes for the wooden floors can be seen. Part of the bawn wall survives to north and east and there is a lintelled channel from the bawn under the wall to a freshwater spring, rising in a small chamber with a corbelled vault.

ASCD 1966, 250–252; McErlean, McConkey and Forsythe, 2002, 103

98 Strangford Castle (J589498)

Location: On a height overlooking the harbour in Strangford town, in Castle Street, across the Strait from Portaferry Castle (**92**). This small tower-house dates from the late 16th century in its present form, but a blocked door of 15th-century type at first floor level suggests the remodelling of an earlier tower. A report in 1540 refers to a castle at Strangford as ruinous and broken down. The present entrance is a reconstruction, positioned by the surviving corbelled machicolation above and a socket for a draw-bar to secure the original door. A simple square in plan, the castle has three floors with no stone vault and no sign of a stone stair. The wooden floors are recent. The first floor fireplace has an oven and dry 'keeping place', and there are window-seats on the first and second floors. Pistol-loops are provided at ground floor level and in the crenellations at roof level.

ASCD 1966, 252–253; D.M. Waterman in *Ulster J. Archaeol.* 30 (1967), 83–86

99 Tullynakill Church (J502645)

Tullynakill Church

Location: 4 miles (6.4km) south-south-east of Comber, between Ballydrain and Ardmillan, approached by a short footpath from a lay-by on the road. Right of the graveyard gate note the low foundations of the 1825 Church of Ireland parish church (demolished in the late 20th century). The old church is of two periods, the late 15th and the early 17th centuries. It replaced Nendrum (**68**), in the late 15th century, as the parish church site and, unusually for Ireland, burial was transferred to the new site and Nendrum was abandoned. The 15th-century church had a west door, but the main visible features are of the 17th century, when the building was 'modernised'. The handsome south door in red Castle Espie limestone, is dated 1639, and of the same period are the windows (all grooved for glass), a two-light east window and three others, the one left of the door surviving particularly well. Although Strangford Lough is not visible, the church is not far from the water and is only 1½ miles (2.4km) west-north-west of Nendrum.

ASCD 1966, 311–312

County Down
Plantation Period and Later Monuments

100 Ballycopeland Windmill (J579761)

Location: 1 mile (1.6km) west of Millisle on the B172. Car park at the site, and displays in the miller's house and kiln range at the approach to the mill. Windmills were once common in grain-growing east Down, but all except Ballycopeland are now ruined. Built in the late 18th or early 19th century, it was worked by the McGilton family until the 1914–1918 war and from the 1950s to 1978 was restored to full working order. It is a tower

Ballycopeland Windmill

mill, the cap with the sails moving on a 'dead curb' and kept into the eye of the wind by the fantail. The top floor has the hoppers into which the grain was emptied, falling to the stones floor below, where there are three pairs of grindstones. Below again is the drive floor where the drive from the central shaft is transferred to the stones, and finally the ground floor where the grain began and ended its journey. Hulls were collected in and cleared from the dust-house adjoining the mill.

PLEASE NOTE: for safety reasons the mill is not normally working. Special arrangements to view the mill in action have to be made with NIEA.

Green 1963, 53, fig. 3; McCutcheon 1980, 227–231 and pl. 46; Donnelly 1997, 128–130

101 Grey Point Fort (J457832)

Location: At Helen's Bay, off Fort Road. For centuries Carrickfergus Castle was responsible for the protection of Belfast Lough and in 1855 it was designated artillery headquarters for Northern Ireland.

Grey Point Fort Battery was established in 1907, closely followed by Kilroot Battery, both manned by the militia formerly at Carrickfergus Castle, the Antrim Artillery.

Grey Point Fort

As the Territorial Army, this special reserve unit continued at Grey Point Fort until 1957, providing 50 years of active service.

The Fort is a hexagonal enclosure within which is a battery armed with two 6 inch breech-loading guns, mark VII, in emplacements 100ft (30m) apart. The store housed three Maxim machine guns. The Battery Observation Post was the tactical command post, best placed to view the situation. Outside the Fort on the shore are three searchlight emplacements, two built in 1936 and one in 1940.

Kerrigan, 1995, 267–269

102 Hillsborough Fort (J245586)

Location: Approached down a tree-lined avenue from the Square, or from the Forest Park car park into the Lake Field south-west of the Fort. Colonel Arthur Hill built this artillery fort in the mid 1600s on the site of an Early Christian period hilltop rath (excavated ditch visible) to command the important route from Dublin to Belfast and Carrickfergus. Later in the century it held a royal garrison, but in the 18th and 19th centuries served a more peaceful purpose as a pleasure

Hillsborough Fort

ground for the Hill family who had moved their main residence to nearby Hillsborough Castle. The Fort is square with spear-shaped angle bastions, the earth bank having its outer face revetted in stone. A rectangular gatehouse in the centre of the north side was

75

remodelled in 1758 in a gothick style (a style that imitated medieval gothic), with four corner towers and a battlemented parapet, and a new entrance in the north-east side was given a gothick gazebo above. Extensive paths link the fort with the Parish Church (1760–1774), the Lake Field and Hillsborough Forest Park. Fine wrought iron gates similar to the ones in front of Hillsborough Castle adorn the entrance from the square.

ASCD 1966, 409–411; C. Gaskell-Brown and N.F. Brannon in *Ulster J. Archaeol.* 41 (1978), 78–87; Donnelly 1997, 125–128; DOENI guide-card 1998

103 Hillsborough Courthouse (Market House) (J243586)

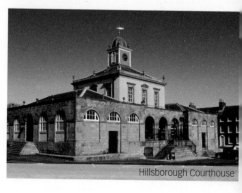
Hillsborough Courthouse

Location: In the town square, built before 1765 as a market house, later used as a courthouse, surrounded by elegant Georgian townhouses. The first building had a two-storey square central block, with an archway from east to west, and single storey covered market arcades on each face. The Grand Jury met in the upper room. In about 1810 the north and south wings were added, one to accommodate a courtroom and the other to form a large market hall. The granite plinth was added, as well as sandstone details – cornices, urns and balls. A new clock and bell were installed in 1810. Today the building provides accommodation for a Tourist Information Centre, an exhibition on 'Law in the Courthouse', and events including markets in the market hall.

ASCD 1966, 411–414; DOENI guide-card 1998

104 Hillsborough: Richhill Gates (J243586)

Richhill Gates

Location: Facing the Courthouse (**103**) at the entrance to Hillsborough Castle, moved from Richhill House, Co. Armagh, in 1936. These fine wrought iron gates and screen were made probably by Cornish immigrants to Armagh, the Thornberry brothers of Falmouth, and were set up at Richhill in 1745. Areas of plain railings are contrasted with exuberantly decorated panels, with an 'overthrow' bearing a coat of arms. The gates were repaired in 1936 and a further major renovation was completed in

1976. Hillsborough Castle, seen through the gates, was built by the Earl of Hillsborough in about 1760, but has been greatly enlarged and altered. Its extensive landscaped grounds contribute to the special atmosphere of Hillsborough, which is a conservation area.

DOENI guide-card 1998

105 Kirkistown Castle (J645580)

Location: 1¼ miles (2km) north-north-east of Cloghy, north-west of the A2 coast road near Ringboy. An off road lay-by is available. The precise date of this castle has been debated recently, and it has been suggested that the main tower dates to the 15th or 16th century, and was refurbished in the 17th century when the bawn was added. As it presently stands, and if one accepts the previously published date of the building, this tower-house displays an unusual combination of 17th-century Gothic survival and 18th-century Gothic revival. Traditional accounts record that it was supposedly built for Roland Savage in 1622, though it is likely that he reused an earlier site. The tower-house is in the medieval tower-house tradition with extra tall parapets. The main bawn still has two round corner towers and part of a second bawn survives, originally a walled garden. The entrance to the tower on its south-east side is protected by a corbelled

Kirkistown Castle

machicolation at roof level. There are three floors, the first floor chambers having pointed stone vaults. Quoins, door and window dressings are in smooth hard limestone. Before 1800 the tower was much altered in Gothic Revival style, acquiring large pointed sash windows, plaster ceilings, gothick fireplaces and new woodwork.

The castle has survived despite all sorts of mistreatment. When first built, the tower had walls of different thicknesses. Internally, an off centre wall carried the pressure of two stone vaults. That wall sank, but what was seen was the bowing of the outside wall. When the late 18th-century work was added, the bottom half of a stone spiral staircase was removed to make way for a flight of stairs – this added to the instability of the outer walls and massive buttresses were added to the south-east face in the 19th century to counter the movement. Over the years the bawn walls gathered a haphazard collection of buttresses and holes. Quarrying beyond the bawn and neglect of the empty castle did further damage. In the 1980s major engineering works were needed to prevent the collapse of the tower, bawn and barn. Following this work the tower has been conserved and the interior has been restored.

ASCD 1966, 238–241

---

106 Shaw's Bridge (J325690)

Location: On the south edge of Belfast, over the River Lagan. Named for Captain Shaw who built a wooden bridge here in 1655 on behalf of Cromwell. The present bridge was built in 1709. In 1976 a new road and bridge were built to take the greater weight of modern traffic, leaving Shaw's Bridge as a monument.

From 1763 the River Lagan was navigable to Lisburn due to the canal works that were being constructed through to Lough Neagh. The bridge, five arches constructed of rubble stone with cutwaters on the south side, leads to tow paths on either side.

Blair 1981, 9–12

---

107 Struell Bath Houses and Wells (J513442)

Location: 1$^1/_2$ miles (2.4km) east of Downpatrick, signposted off the B1 (Ardglass) road and reached down a long lane to a small car park. This is an early (probably pre- AD 1000) site, though most of the upstanding elements here today are more recent. The site is rich in traditions and strongly associated with St Patrick, but the earliest written reference is in 1302–1306 and none of the surviving buildings is certainly earlier than about 1600. A fast-flowing stream runs, partly underground, through

Struell Bath Houses and Wells

the secluded, rocky valley and along it are ranged five buildings. Furthest north-west is the gaunt shell of a mid 18th-century church, apparently never finished. This must have replaced an earlier church: a chapel was listed here in the 1302–1306 taxation roll. Nearby is the Drinking Well, circular with a domed vault built on wicker centring.

The Eye Well is rectangular with a pyramidal corbelled stone roof. To the south-east the stone-roofed Men's Bathhouse has a dressing room with seats leading to the bath-room with its tank. A third room, also with seats, served as a dressing room to the adjoining Women's Bathhouse, now roofless. Pilgrimages to the site are well documented from the 16th to 19th centuries.

R.H. Buchanan in *Ulster J. Archaeol.* 19 (1956), 92–112; *ASCD* 1966, 310–311; Donnelly 1997, 123–125

108 The White House, Ballyspurge (J643550)

Location: ³/₄ mile (1.2km) south-east of Cloghy, on a slope overlooking Slanes Bay, approached by a long lane through the caravan site to the south and on foot uphill from the end of the lane. The building is known to have been in use by the 1640s, when it was associated with a Patrick Savage. It is unclear when it was first built, as there are few similar structures elsewhere in Ulster. This gabled house is an unusual survival, combining defensive with more purely domestic features. Rectangular in plan and one and a half storeys high, it has thick walls with pistol-loops, but the windows are large and the general appearance is domestic rather than defensive. There are fireplaces in the gable walls. Attached to the west corner of the house was a bawn, of which remnants of two sides survive, including the remains of a gatehouse to the south-west.

E.M. Jope in *Ulster J. Archaeol.* 23 (1960), esp. 107; *ASCD* 1966, 256–259

The White House

PREHISTORIC MONUMENTS

109. Aghanaglack Dual Court Tomb (H098436)
110. Drumskinny Stone Circle, Cairn and
Alignment (H201707)

EARLY CHRISTIAN PERIOD AND
MEDIEVAL MONUMENTS

111. Aghalurcher Church (H365314)
112. Devenish Ecclesiastical Site (H224469)
113. Inishmacsaint Church and Cross (H165541)
114. White Island Church and Figures (H175600)

PLANTATION PERIOD MONUMENTS

115. Castle Balfour (H362337)
116. Enniskillen Castle (H231442)
117. Monea Castle (H164493)
118. Old Castle Archdale (H186599
119. Portora Castle (H222345)
120. Tully Castle (H126566)

17

30

County Fermanagh
Prehistoric Monuments

109 Aghanaglack Dual Court Tomb (H098436)

Location: 3¼ miles (5.2km) north-north-east of Belcoo, approached from the road from Belcoo to Boho. Turn north-west to Aghanaglack Forest and along a (signposted) forest road, parking close to the monument and walking the short remaining distance. The tomb is built across the slope on a south-east-facing mountainside. Until the 1950s this was open grazing land with a farmhouse beside the monument, but it is now forested. It was excavated by Oliver Davies in 1938, but had been much disturbed by earlier

Aghanaglack Dual Court Tomb

excavation, reuse of stone for building and use as a pigsty. Davies found structural features, especially of the cairn kerb, which are now overgrown and invisible. This is, nevertheless, a fine example of a dual court tomb, with two two-chambered galleries sharing a common backstone. The court to the south-west is roughly semicircular but has been disturbed. It opens into two chambers built of huge limestone slabs. The north-east court is a half oval in shape and the two chambers are made of smaller stones. Finds included small fragments of burned bone of a child or children and the burned remains of a youth. There were also some animal bones, plain and decorated Neolithic bowls, flint implements and a stone bead. Two barbed and tanged flint arrowheads indicate some early Bronze Age activity here.

O. Davies in *J. Roy. Soc. Antiq. Ireland* 69 (1939), 21–38; *PSAMNI* 1940, 159; Herity 1987, esp. 214–216 and fig. 37

110 Drumskinny Stone Circle, Cairn and Alignment (H201707)

Location: 4½ miles (7.2km) north of Kesh, east of the minor road north to Castlederg. Car park close to the monument. The site lies in upland bog and was drained after excavation in 1962. A circle 12.8m in diameter is made up of 39 stones, and a small round cairn is associated with an alignment, 7.6m long, of 24 stones. The stones are fairly small and some replaced after the excavation are clearly marked. It is far smaller but of the same general type as Beaghmore circles (**154**) and many others in mid-Ulster. Finds were sparse but included Neolithic material, so it is not clear whether the site dates from the Neolithic or the Bronze Age. There are other prehistoric stone monuments in the bog in this area.

D.M. Waterman in *Ulster J. Archaeol.* 27 (1964), 23–30; Donnelly 1997, 33–34

Drumskinny Stone Circle

County Fermanagh
Early Christian Period and Medieval Monuments

111 Aghalurcher Church (H365314)

Location: 1¹/₂ miles (2.4km) south of Lisnaskea. This is the site of an early church, founded probably in the 7th century by St Ronan, but the visible ruins are of the medieval parish church. This was substantial, as the foundations of the east end show, but it is badly ruined. The church was patronised by the Maguires, whose main burial place was here. In 1447 Thomas Maguire put a 'French roof' (perhaps a ribbed vault) on the church and rebuilt the east gable. There are many fine gravestones, some protected in the covered vault on the north side of the church. Two 12th-century stones from the site, a slab showing a bishop with a crosier and a book, and an exhibitionist corbel, are displayed at Fermanagh County Museum in Enniskillen. A surprising recent discovery at this site is the medieval stone carving on both of the gate pillars at the entrance to the graveyard. These include a crucifixion scene along with a number of figures carved in relief on the faces of the pillars that were formerly built into the graveyard wall. These were only discovered after the pillars were moved following the collapse of an arch that used to span the entrance to the site.

Aghalurcher Church

G. Dagg in *J. Roy. Soc. Antiq. Ireland* 24 (1894), 264–270; Hickey 1985, 56–58 and 72–73

112 Devenish Ecclesiastical Site (H224469)

Location: Island site at the south end of Lower Lough Erne, 1¹/₂ miles (2.4km) downstream from Enniskillen. A ferry runs from Trory Point in the summer, reached along the lane to the lough shore (car park) from the junction of the B82 to Kesh with the A32 to Ballinamallard (not suitable for large buses). Cruisers also run from Enniskillen. The most important of Lough Erne's many island church settlements, Devenish was founded in the 6th century by St Molaise. It was raided by Vikings in 837 and burned in 1157, but in the Middle Ages flourished as the site of the parish church and St Mary's Augustinian Priory. There are extensive low earthworks on the hillside, but the earliest buildings are St Molaise's House (a very small church) and the fine round tower close by, both with accomplished Romanesque decoration of the 12th century. *Teampull Mór*, the lower church, dates from the early 13th century with a beautifully moulded south window. It

Devenish Ecclesiastical Site

was extended to the east in about 1300, and later additions include a residential wing to the north and the Maguire Chapel to the south, with 17th-century heraldic slabs. St

Mary's Augustinian Priory on the hilltop is of the mid 15th and early 16th centuries, with church, tower and small north cloister. In its graveyard stands an unusual, intricately-carved cross of the mid 15th century. There are several hundred loose architectural fragments on the site and among them are more than 40 stones from an otherwise unknown, richly-decorated Romanesque church. In the small visitor centre some of the many loose stones are displayed and set in their historical context.

C.A.R. Radford in *Ulster J. Archaeol.* 33 (1970), 55–62 (with further references); D.M. Waterman in Ulster J. Archaeol 42 (1979), 34–50; Hickey 1985, 51–52 and 63–70; PoP 1988, 52–54; Donnelly 1997, 53–56; Lalor 1999, 142–145; A. Hamlin and R. Stalley in *Ulster J. Archaeol.* 61 (2002) 83–97

Devenish Ecclesiastical Site

County Fermanagh
Early Christian Period and Medieval Monuments

> 113 Inishmacsaint Church and Cross (H165541)

Location: Island near the west shore of Lower Lough Erne off Ross Point, 7½ miles (12km) north-west of Enniskillen off the A46. No ferry service but there is a jetty close to the site at the south-east corner of the island. St Ninnid founded a church here in the 6th century, and the site was later used for the parish church and graveyard, being abandoned for the mainland only in the 18th century. The ruined church is of two main periods: the west

Inishmacsaint Church and Cross

end represents a small pre-Romanesque church of perhaps the 10th or 11th century, with a blocked west door, and the east end is an extension dating from around 1200, with a small south window altered in the 15th century. South-west of the church is a tall unringed cross, the head separately worked and attached to the shaft by a mortice and tenon joint. The cross is plain except for slight traces of panels on the head and it is very difficult to date. A pre 12th-century date is possible but not certain.

PSAMNI 1940, 153; Gwynn and Hadcock 1970, 38; Harbison 1992, 100, 376 and fig. 325

114 White Island Church and Figures (H175600)

Location: In Castle Archdale Bay, near the east shore of Lower Lough Erne, reached from the B82. A ferry usually runs from the marina in Castle Archdale Country Park during the main visitor season. A small ruined church dating from around 1200 lies within the large earthwork enclosure of a pre-Norman church. Nothing is known of the early history of the establishment, and even its early name is forgotten, but one early grave slab is exhibited at the site and another has been reported. The main feature of the church is its late Romanesque south door, reconstructed from a ruined state in 1928. The stone figures set up against the north wall pre-date the church, and may belong to an earlier church. Depressions cut into the tops of the heads of the figures may have been used to secure or support a timber structure. There has been much discussion of the symbolism of the figures. They include a cleric with a bell and crosier and there is no doubt that they are Christian in significance, not pagan. A 9th- or 10th-century date seems likely.

D. Lowry-Corry, B.C.S. Wilson and D.M. Waterman in *Ulster J. Archaeol.* 22 (1959), 59–66; Hickey 1985, 26–30 and 35–42

White Island Church and Figures

County Fermanagh
Plantation Period Monuments

---

115 Castle Balfour (H362337)

Castle Balfour

Location: In Lisnaskea, at the edge of the parish graveyard west of the main street, approached through the graveyard. The view from the housing estate south of the castle gives an idea of its defensive strength. The castle was built from about 1618 onwards by the Scottish planter, Sir James Balfour, and shows clear Scottish influence in plan and details. It was altered in 1652 and damaged in 1689 but continued in occupation until the early 19th century. Major conservation was done in the 1960s and in the late 1990s. A wing formerly projecting east into the graveyard has disappeared. The surviving building is of T- plan with the entrance through a dressed-stone projecting bay with gun-loops. On the ground floor are vaulted rooms and a kitchen with remains of a large fireplace and small oven. The main dwelling rooms were at first floor level and the stairs to rooms above are carried in a corbelled-out turret made of sharply cut grey limestone. There are Balfour grave slabs in the vault at Aghalurcher Church (**111**)

The Earl of Erne in *Ulster J. Archaeol.* 2 (1896), 79–95; D.M. Waterman in *Ulster J. Archaeol.* 31 (1968), 71–76

---

116 Enniskillen Castle (H231442)

Enniskillen Castle

Location: On the south-west corner of Enniskillen island, approached from the main street by Castle Street or Wesley Street. Hugh Maguire built the first castle here in the early 15th century to command the Erne waterway. Part of the keep may date from that period. A focus of Irish resistance to the English in the 16th century, the castle was much involved in warfare and fell after an eight-day siege in 1594. In 1607 Captain William Cole was appointed constable and refurbished and remodelled the castle. The keep was repaired and the Watergate was added (not in fact a gate, but a tower fronting the Erne). In the late 18th

Enniskillen Castle

century the complex was remodelled as the Castle Barracks. The castle complex houses the Fermanagh County Museum and the Regimental Museum of the Royal Inniskilling Fusiliers, along with displays about monuments in Fermanagh in the curved barrack range.

E.M. Jope in *Ulster J. Archaeol.* 14 (1951), 32–47; Lanigan Wood 1990

County Fermanagh
Plantation Period Monuments

Location: 3 miles (4.8km) south-east of Derrygonnelly, 1/2 mile (0.8km) east of Monea Church of Ireland church, approached along a wooded drive through Castletown demesne. This is the finest of Fermanagh's Plantation castles, built from 1618–1619 for Malcolm Hamilton. Captured in the 1641 rising, it was refurbished and used until gutted by fire in the mid 18th century. The walled bawn is much ruined. It has two flanker towers, the one beside the entrance once used for housing pigeons. The castle at the south-east corner of the bawn survives almost to full height though lacking its roofs. The entrance front (west) has two circular towers capped with square chambers with crow-stepped gables, similar to a site at Claypotts near Dundee (in Scotland). On the ground floor were vaulted rooms and a kitchen, with hall and chambers above. The castle

Monea Castle

is well provided with gun-loops. A clump of trees in the partly-drained lake to the south marks a crannóg. In the field between the car park and the castle are the earthworks of the castle garden.

E.M. Jope in *Ulster J. Archaeol.* 14 (1951), 32–34; Dixon 1975, 18

118 Old Castle Archdale (H186599)

Location: In Castle Archdale Forest Park, close to the junction of the B72 and B82 roads, near the east shore of Lower Lough Erne on a small defensive hill. Car park nearby. These are the remains of a T-shaped house and bawn built for the English planter, John Archdale, on land granted in 1612. Captured in 1641, the castle was repaired but finally burned and abandoned in 1689. Little survives of the bawn except part of the south wall with its wall-walk and a semicircular-headed gate. Above this on the outside is a Latin inscription recording the construction by John Archdale in 1615. The house occupies the north end of the bawn, above a steep slope. It is very fragmentary and heavily restored but probably had two storeys with attics. Parts of the east gable and south wall survive, but the main fragment is the projecting north tower, three storeys high, which held a wooden stair,

Old Castle Archdale

defended with gun-loops and lit by square-headed, three-light windows at a higher level. The castle is generally English in design, but there are signs of Scottish influence in the details of the bawn gateway.

D.M. Waterman in *Ulster J. Archaeol.* 22 (1959), 119–123

County Fermanagh
Plantation Period Monuments

---

119 Portora Castle (H222345)

Location: 1 mile (1.6km) north-west of Enniskillen, reached by turning right from the A46 (Donegal to Belleek) road on the outskirts of the town and along a track towards the lough to a car park at the site. The castle guards a former crossing point of the Erne, where the river joins the open lough, important since prehistoric times. It was built in 1613 by Sir William Cole and Pynnar describes it in 1619 as a bawn with four flankers and a house or castle of three storeys high 'strongly wrought'. Between 1621 and 1628 it was lived in by James Spottiswood, Bishop of Clogher. The castle had an important military role in the 1641 rising and again in 1688. In 1859 part of the castle was blown up by boys of Portora School, and more of it fell in the great gale of 1893–1894. The two tall round towers to the north and west were integrated with the house, which occupied one side of the bawn. They have splayed gun-loops for defence and there are traces of fireplaces in the house wall, but little survives of its other walls. The east flanker tower was lost to river dredging works, but the south tower still stands, lower than those linked to the house. Excavation in the bawn in the 1990s showed that very few archaeological remains survived. There is an impressive view of the castle from boats passing through the lock below.

E.M. Jope, *Ulster J. Archaeol.* 21 (1958), 107–108

Portora Castle

120 Tully Castle (H126566)

Location: Above the west shore of Lower Lough Erne, 3 miles (4.8km) north of Derrygonnelly, approached by a lane off the A46 lough shore road between Enniskillen and Belleek. Turn right into large car park and approach the castle past the small visitor centre. The castle is beautifully sited on a hill overlooking the lough; there is a path around the headland and a jetty close by. The fortified house and bawn were built for the Scottish planter, Sir John Hume, following his land grant in 1610, but were captured and burned on Christmas Eve, 1641 by Rory Maguire; its inhabitants were later massacred. It was never lived in again. The rectangular bawn with four rectangular angle towers is ruined low to the west but survives to some height to the east. An interesting feature of the bawn is extensive original paving, uncovered during the

Tully Castle

conservation work. The house survives to almost full height of two storeys with attics. The ground floor room is vaulted (notice the marks of the wicker centring) with a large fireplace. A wooden stair against the east wall of the projecting entrance tower led to the main accommodation above. The upper north angles are carried up as projecting circular towers, not built of cut stone, as at Castle Balfour, but of rubble, originally plastered. The T-plan is Scottish in inspiration but Irish masons probably carried out the work. The spacing of the gable stones indicate a thatched roof. A garden with plants known to have existed in 17th-century Ireland has been created within the framework of the paving in the bawn. There was a village for 24 families near the castle in the early 17th century. An early path leading down to a nearby farm (where the visitor centre is now) may indicate the site of this village. Another path leading towards the water passes an old well.

D.M. Waterman in *Ulster J. Archaeol.* 22 (1959), 123–126; Donnelly 1997, 114–116

PREHISTORIC MONUMENTS

121. Ballybriest Dual Court Tomb: Carnanbane (H762886)
121. Ballybriest Wedge Tomb (H762885)
123. Ballygroll Prehistoric Landscape (C533137 and area)
124. Ervey Portal Tomb (C517126)
125. Knockoneill Court Tomb (C819087)
126. Mobuy 'Standing Stone' (H783859)
127. Mount Sandel Mesolithic Site (C854307)
128. Mullaboy Standing Stone (C516130)
129. Tamnyrankin Court Tomb (C834102)
130. Tirnony Dolmen (C841017)

EARLY CHRISTIAN PERIOD AND MEDIEVAL MONUMENTS

131. Ballintemple Bullaun Stone (C811149)
132. Ballynascreen Church (H730907)
133. Banagher Church (C676066)
134. Bovevagh Church (C667141)
135. Church Island, Lough Beg (H9752 9464)
136. Drum Fort, also known as Larry's Fort (C654113)
137. Dunalis Souterrain (C804306)
138. Dungiven Priory (C692083)
139. Gortycavan Mound (C791315)
140. Inishrush Crannog (C937042)
141. Maghera Church (C855002)
142. Mill Loughan Mound (C876292)
143. Mountsandel Fort (C853307)
144. O'Cahan's Castle (C679203)
145. Tullyheran Fort (C835017)

PLANTATION PERIOD AND LATER MONUMENTS

146. Bellaghy Bawn (H953963)
147. Brackfield Bawn or Crossalt (C511097)
148. Derry's Walls (C435167 and area)
149. Magilligan Martello Tower (C660388)
150. Tirkane Sweat House (C827025)

County Londonderry
Prehistoric Monuments

121 Ballybriest Dual Court Tomb: Carnanbane (H762886)

Location: On the lower west slopes of Slieve Gallion, overlooking Lough Fea to the south-west, approached from the B41 south-west from Draperstown or the B162 north-west from Cookstown and the minor road over the high ground east of Lough Fea. This dual court tomb is unfortunately damaged, cut almost in half down the long axis of the cairn.

Ballybriest Dual Court Tomb

Originally at each end, east and west, a semicircular court led to a short, two-chambered burial gallery. Excavation in 1937 showed that there were Neolithic flints, pottery, burned bone, charcoal and a cremation burial under the cairn, and pits were sealed under this layer. The excavator interpreted this as evidence of ritual at the time of the building of the tomb, but it is possible that there was domestic activity on the site at an earlier period in the Neolithic. This and the following monument form elements in an extensive prehistoric landscape, with many sites of the Neolithic and Bronze Age, a landscape sadly now greatly altered and damaged by quarrying activity.

E.E .Evans in *Proc. Roy. Irish Acad.* 45C (1939), 1–12; Herity 1987, esp. 186–194 and figs 26–28

122 Ballybriest Wedge Tomb (H762885)

Location: Close to Carnanbane (**121**), about 300 feet (91.5m) to the south, downslope in bogland. Megalithic tomb, only partly cut out of the peat, orientated to the south-west, with two large capstones in place on side and end stones. A small excavation in 1970 did not find out much about the site, but it is certainly a wedge tomb, similar to another example nearby, excavated in 1997, which produced Beaker pottery of the early Bronze Age.

Ballybriest Wedge Tomb

PSAMNI 1940, 212; D.P Hurl in *Ulster J. Archaeol.* 60 (2001)

123 Ballygroll Prehistoric Landscape (C533137 and area)

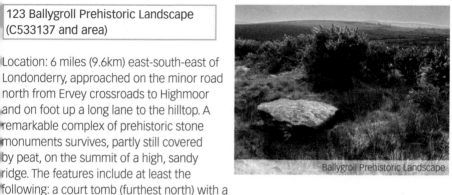
Ballygroll Prehistoric Landscape

Location: 6 miles (9.6km) east-south-east of Londonderry, approached on the minor road north from Ervey crossroads to Highmoor and on foot up a long lane to the hilltop. A remarkable complex of prehistoric stone monuments survives, partly still covered by peat, on the summit of a high, sandy ridge. The features include at least the following: a court tomb (furthest north) with a disturbed, cup-marked capstone, several wedge tombs, two stone circles, several cairns, and many stretches of stone field walls. The date of the walls is uncertain (possibly Iron Age), but the megalithic monuments extend from the Neolithic period into the Bronze Age. Excavation was done in 1978–1979 on a barrow and a field wall in the context of land reclamation. An area of 11 acres is in state care, but this is only a small part of the prehistoric landscape on the south and west flanks of Loughermore Mountain, recorded since the 1830s but now largely swept away by agricultural reclamation.

O. Davies in *Ulster J. Archaeol.* 9 (1948), 48–53; B.B. Williams in *Ulster J. Archaeol.* 44–45 (1981–1982), 29–46; Neill 1999, 63–64

124 Ervey Portal Tomb (C517126)

Every Portal Tomb

Location: 3¹/₂ miles (5.6km) north-north-west of Claudy and ¹/₃ mile (0.5km) north-north-west of Ervey crossroads, east of a minor road. This monument stands on a sheltered platform in the south-east corner of a field and can be interpreted as a well-preserved portal tomb facing east. Two portal stones and a low sill stone at the east end lead to a chamber with long side stones and a back stone. Two fallen stones may be former capstones. This is part of the concentration of prehistoric monuments noted in this area (see **123** and **128**).

PSAMNI 1940, 199; Ó Nualláin 1983, 80 and 93

County Londonderry
Prehistoric Monuments

Knockoneill Court Tomb

Location: 2¼ miles (3.6km) west-north-west of Swatragh, reached by turning west in the south outskirts of Swatragh and driving west-north-west up the mountain and taking a left turn towards Tamnybrack. This complex tomb is north-west of Tamnybrack, in the east fringes of the Sperrins, on the north-east slope of Carntogher, with extensive views to the east and south. The long cairn encloses two chambers, with an ante-chamber and a court at the north-west end. At the back of the chambers another chamber is approached by a passage from the side of the cairn on the south-east. Many of the stones which revetted the cairn are visible. Excavations in 1948, 1977 and 1983 are not fully published, but finds included Neolithic and Bronze Age pottery in the main chambers and a cremation and pits with pottery in the court. The monument shows some features of wedge tombs, and possibly the site was turned into a Bronze Age round cairn. Clearly there was activity over a long period, from the Neolithic into the Bronze Age.

I. Herring in *Archaeol. Newsletter* 9 (1949), 7–8; L.N.W. Flanagan in *Ulster J. Archaeol.* 43 (1980), 9–14; C.S. Briggs in *Ulster J. Archaeol.* 46 (1983), 23–27; Herity 1987, esp. 242–243 and fig. 27

Mobuy Standing Stone

Location: 2 miles (3.2km) south-east of Ballybriest megaliths (**121** and **122**), 1 mile (1.6km) north-north-east of Lissan on the lower south-west slopes of Slieve Gallion. A single stone stands on a level area on the hillside, according to local memory the last of a ring of eight or ten stones known as the 'Druids Circle'. Early accounts suggest that this may be the last remaining stone of a court tomb, but without excavation it is not possible to be sure.

Neill 1999, 39 and 49

127 Mount Sandel Mesolithic Site (C854307)

Location: 1¼ miles (2km) south-south-east of Coleraine, close to the north-east of Mountsandel Fort (143), between the woodland and 1970s housing. Beyond the Mound, the site is close to the River Bann. The fence encloses the main area of the important Mesolithic site, excavated between 1973 and 1977. The post-holes, pits and hearths of the settlement were investigated, as well as evidence for the economy and technology of the people who camped there. Mount Sandel is one of the earliest known sites in Ireland where traces of buildings survive from over 8,000 years ago. Peter Woodman and his team distinguished three or four separate zones: a living area; a work area where flint tools were made and tens of thousands of flints were found; and an area with deep rubbish pits.

Nothing is visible above ground, but the area is marked as a monument to remind us of the size and place of this great discovery.

Woodman 1983; *PoP* 1988, 1–2; Donnelly 1997, 9–10

128 Mullaboy Standing Stone (C516130)

Location: ⅓ mile (0.5km) north-north-west of Ervey court tomb (124) and 1¼ miles (2km) east-south-east of Ballygroll (123), immediately west of a minor road. A tall fallen stone lies with its long axis north-south. Stones around it may be the remains of a cairn or could result from field clearance, but without excavation it is impossible to be sure whether this was a solitary standing stone or part of a megalithic tomb.

Mullaboy Standing Stone

County Londonderry
Prehistoric Monuments

129 Tamnyrankin Court Tomb (C834102)

Location: 2½ miles (4km) north-west of Swatragh, reached by turning west off the A29 north of Swatragh on Tamnyrankin Road and then right along a lane to a lay-by. There are magnificent views from the site all around except to the south-west. This is a fine court tomb with a long, high cairn, a semicircular court on the south-east, defined by

Tamnyrankin Court Tomb

impressive stones, and probably a two-chambered gallery (only one chamber is exposed). At the back of the cairn is an unusual subsidiary gallery across its whole width, with an antechamber to the north-east and jambs defining two chambers. This feature was excavated in 1939–1940 and further work on the tomb was done in 1977. The gallery was badly disturbed but some cremated bone was found as well as several different types of pottery and flints, indicating both Neolithic and Bronze Age activity.

I. Herring in *J. Roy. Soc. Antiq. Ireland* 71 (1941), 31–52; Herity 1987, esp. 195–198 and figs 29–30

130 Tirnony Dolmen (C841017)

Location: 1 mile (1.6km) north-west of Maghera, close to (east of) the minor road from Maghera to Tirkane. This fine portal tomb stands on the margins of the higher land, lower than the court tombs to the north (**125** and **129**). It faces north-east and the huge, sloping capstone is supported on two tall portal stones, four side stones and an end stone. The

Tirnony Dolmen

stone on the right of the entrance hints at the start of a court in the court tomb tradition. Tirkane sweat house (**150**) is 1 mile (1.6km) to the north-west.

PSAMNI 1940, 209; Ó Nualláin 1983, 80 and 93; Neill 1999, 39–40

County Londonderry
Early Christian Period and Medieval Monuments

131 Ballintemple Bullaun Stone (C811149)

Location: 2 miles (3.2km) west-south-west of Garvagh on the B64 to Dungiven, beside the farmhouse immediately south of Errigal graveyard. This was the site of a pre-Norman church and the medieval parish church of Errigal. The bullaun stone must survive from the pre-Norman occupation: a large basalt boulder with a hollow, often water-filled and regarded as a font, but probably a mortar for grinding food and other materials. In the field north of the graveyard is a rock-cut souterrain (not in state care), another sign of Early Christian period activity in this area.

PSAMNI 1940, 197

132 Ballynascreen Church (H730907)

Ballynascreen Church

Location: 4 miles (6.4km) south-west of Draperstown by the B41, continuing straight on the Sixtowns Road then right to Moneyconey Bridge and over the river. Access is along a path between fields to a stile into the graveyard. The church, in Moneyconey townland, stands beside the river in the lovely Moyola valley. It is traditionally associated with St Columba (Colmcille) and there must have been an early church here. It is documented as the medieval parish church, but it was ruined by 1622. The long ruin is difficult to date and there are no dressed stones in place except for a niche in the east wall which has a delicate miniature ribbed vault. The present door is a ragged gap in the south wall with a draw-bar hole, but built into the wall near it are many pieces of a fine moulded door of the 13th century, reused as building material. This points to extensive rebuilding, perhaps in the 15th century. In the walls are many putlog holes for scaffolding poles.

O. Davies in *Ulster J. Archaeol.* 4 (1941), 57–63

County Londonderry
Early Christian Period and Medieval Monuments

133 Banagher Church (C676066)

Mortuary House at Banagher Church

Location: In Magheramore townland, 2 miles (3.2km) south-south-west of Dungiven, approached from the B74 to Feeny or the minor road south from the centre of Dungiven through Turmeel. The church, on a prominent hill of sand and gravel, was traditionally founded by St Muiredach O'Heney who may have lived in the late 11th or early 12th century. It is first mentioned in 1121. This was the medieval parish church, chosen by Archbishop Colton of Armagh as the base for his visitation of Derry diocese in 1397, but abandoned in the 17th century. The nave must date from the early or mid 12th century (the date 474 on the west door was cut in the 1730s). There is a small semicircular-headed south window and a fine west door, archaic in general appearance, with a massive lintel and sloping jambs, but with a semicircular arch inside.

Banagher Church

The chancel was added in the early 13th century, with three windows, the south with elegant multiple roll mouldings, and a similarly moulded *sedile* (seat) in the south wall. This was blocked when the east end was remodelled in the 15th century to form a narrow sacristy behind the altar. Unfortunately after excavation the 15th-century features had to be covered again to prevent rapid weathering. The exterior east angles have attached shafts with decorated capitals, reset at a lower level than their original eaves height. south-west of the chancel, in the same distinctive masonry, is the small church- or house-shaped mortuary house, traditionally St Muiredach's burial place. This is the source of the famous Banagher sand which can bring good fortune to members of the saint's family. East of the church is a simple stone cross and a bullaun stone (outside the graveyard wall), and a second cross stands across the road to the south-west on the townland boundary. The ruin west of the graveyard gate is the remains of the medieval priest's strong-house or tower, still standing to gable height in the early 19th century.

D.M. Waterman in *Ulster J. Archaeol.* 23 (1960), 82–88 and 39 (1976), 25–41

134 Bovevagh Church (C667141)

Bovevagh Church

Location: 3 miles (4.8km) north-north-west of Dungiven, reached by a turning west off the B192, on a hill above the Bovevagh River. This was the site of a pre-Norman church (a timber church – *dertech* – stood here in 1100) and of the medieval parish church. The present church ruin is medieval with later alterations, and although reported as ruined in 1622, it was repaired and used until the 19th century. It was entered by a south door and windows remain in the north, south and west walls. Near its south-west corner is a small mortuary house or saint's grave, with a body-shaped cavity and hand-hole at the east end for access to the relics. Of rubble construction with a stone slab roof, it is simpler than the Banagher tomb (**133**) but is of the same general type. A third in the county can be seen at Tamlaghtard, east of Bellarena station (C677313), with a ruined medieval church and holy well nearby.

PSAMNI 1940, 200; D.M. Waterman in *Ulster J. Archaeol.* 23 (1960), 82–88

135 Church Island, Lough Beg (H9752 9464)

Location: The small island in Lough Beg can be viewed from the Strand 3 miles (4.8km) south-east of Bellaghy. In the summer one can walk over the bog meadows to it, otherwise a boat from Newferry at the north of the lake would be needed. The island appears to have been in use at virtually every period starting from the late Mesolithic. The ruins of a rectangular medieval church and graveyard still attract an annual pilgrimage. Bishop Harvey added a tower and spire in 1788 to enhance the view from his house, Ballyscullion, overlooking the lake.

136 Drum Fort, also known as Larry's Fort (C654113)

Location: 2½ miles (4km) north-west of Dungiven, overlooking a tributary of the River Roe, approached on farm lanes. This is a large rath, perhaps originally bivallate, but now with a single bank to the north, upslope, and a bank, ditch and outer bank to the south, downslope. The interior is much disturbed by cultivation and the *Ordnance Survey Memoir* reports that a former tenant levelled and carried away much of the fort for manure. An underground structure described as a drain may be a souterrain, though its size is not clear.

Day, McWilliams and Dobson 1994, 10

County Londonderry
Early Christian Period and Medieval Monuments

137 Dunalis Souterrain (C804306)

Location: 3 miles west-south-west of Coleraine, on the west side of Dunalis Reservoir. The souterrain is capped and is only opened by arrangement with NIEA. It was discovered and excavated in 1934. Three chambers, at slightly different levels, are linked by narrow 'creeps' and a long transverse chamber beyond is filled in and not accessible. Souterrain ware, a kind of early medieval pottery, was found in the excavation. There is a faintly scratched Ogham inscription on one of the lintels in the second chamber, one of only seven known in Northern Ireland.

W.A. Lindsay in *Proc. Belfast Nat. Hist. Phil. Soc.* (1934–5), 61–70; Macalister 1945, 304; Evans 1966, 151

138 Dungiven Priory (C692083)

Location: Reached on foot down a long lane south-west from the A6 at the east approach to Dungiven. The graveyard and ruined church stand on a promontory high above the River Roe. A pre-Norman church associated with St Nechtan was succeeded in the late 12th century by a priory of Augustinian Canons, closely associated with the O'Cahans who, by the late Middle Ages, appear to have had a castle on the site, possibly the tower

Dungiven Priory

attached to the west end of the church. After the suppression of the priory the buildings were remodelled in the early 17th century by Sir Edward Doddington to create a grand house and bawn, and the church was refurbished. The house had almost completely disappeared but its site was excavated in 1982, revealing a domestic complex built within the precinct of the former priory. Raven's view of 1622 shows the church still roofed and the house with a formal garden on the western slope.

15th Century Tomb at Dungiven Priory

The church shows work of many periods. Earliest is the nave with its south window, contemporary with Banagher nave (133) (early or mid 12th century). The fine chancel, originally stone-vaulted, was added in the 13th century and against its south wall is an ornate 15th-century tomb, traditionally of Cooey-na-Gall O'Cahan, who died in 1385. The gallowglasses, Scottish mercenaries, carved on the tomb suggest that it was probably carved by a western Scottish craftsman. There are traces of the early 17th-century refurbishing, especially in the chancel arch and north door and porch. The bullaun beside the path to the church is visited for wart cures.

O. Davies in *Ulster J. Archaeol.* 2 (1939), 271–287 (dating requires revision); N.F. Brannon and B.S. Blades in *Ulster J. Archaeol.* 43 (1980), 91–96; *PoP* 1988, 81–84; Hamlin 2001

139 Gortycavan Mound (C791315)

Location: 3¹/₂ miles (5.6km) west-south-west of Coleraine, on the east side of a minor road between the A2 and B201, one field from the road, on a ridge with extensive views north-east to the Bann estuary. The mound, with a slightly dished summit, has traces of a bank round its edge and is surrounded by a ditch and outer bank. Though somewhat like a motte, it is likely to be a pre-Norman raised rath, dating to the first millennium AD. A mound in Big Glebe 2¹/₂ miles (4km) north-west, now levelled, was shown by excavation to be pre-Norman.

PoP 1988, 41–44 for Big Glebe excavation

140 Inishrush Crannóg (C937042)

Location: 2 miles (3.2km) west of Portglenone, visible to the north of the minor road just west of Claudy Roman Catholic church. The site of the crannóg is marked by a small cluster of trees and bushes in the expanse of bog which is the largely-drained Green Lough. There was interest in the site in the 19th century, as it was believed that it had been the 17th-century base of Brian Carrach O'Neill. The lough was about a mile in circumference but was drained (some years before 1860). An eminence of clay and gravel with a circle of oak piles supporting horizontal timbers was reported, but it seems that the crannóg was largely dismantled in the 19th century. The site cannot be safely approached across the bog and should be viewed only from the adjoining road.

W. Reeves and W.J. Knowles in *Ulster J. Archaeol.* 10 (1904), 29–30 and 54

141 Maghera Church (C855002)

Location: On the east outskirts of the town in Largantogher townland, near the approach by the A42. There are parking facilities near the graveyard gate, and a key is usually available from the nearby recreation centre. St Lurach founded an important church here in the 6th century. It was plundered by Vikings in 832 and burned in 1135. Following the 12th-century ecclesiastical reforms this was the seat of a bishop from the mid 12th to the mid 13th century, then served as parish church until the new church across the road was built in the early 19th century. This long history is reflected in the much patched and altered fabric, and the big uneven graveyard.

The earliest part of the church is the nave, built of large, unevenly-sized stones and with traces of *antae*. It is perhaps as early as the 10th century. The fine west door, now under the added tower, probably dates to the mid 12th century. This door is of the same structural type as the Banagher door (**133**), with a lintel outside (under the tower) and a semicircular arch within. The outer face is elaborately

Maghera Church

carved with Romanesque decoration: interlace, floral and animal motifs on the jambs and a crowded crucifixion scene on the lintel, with Christ flanked by the thieves and 11 other figures, perhaps representations of his disciples, with angels above the cross. The chancel may have been added in about 1200 and there are signs of later medieval and post-medieval alterations to the windows. The tower was added in the 17th century. West of the church, prominently sited in the graveyard, is a rough pillar stone with a carved ringed cross, visible only in good diagonal light. This is traditionally St Lurach's burial place.

O. Davies in *Proc. Belfast Nat. Hist. Phil. Soc.* 2 (1940–45), 17–22; Gwynn and Hadcock 1970, 93; McNab 1987, 19–33

142 Mill Loughan Mound (C876292)

Location: 3 miles south-south-east of Coleraine, on the west side of the minor road which runs beside the River Bann. Entrance is on a narrow stretch of road so best to park a little further north and walk back (taking care of passing traffic). This fine mound stands on a height above the Bann valley, watching over this important route. This may be a motte of the Anglo-Norman invasion period (late 12th or early 13th century), but its profile is markedly rounded and without excavation it is impossible to be sure of its date. The mound is about 3.75m high and there is a surrounding ditch about 4m wide. Traces of an external bank survive on the west, south and east, but there is no sign of a claimed 'bailey'. This mound is in an area with several medieval monuments, including a church, but the early church site of Camus is just across the river.

PSAMNI 1940, 190; T.E. McNeill in *Ulster J. Archaeol.* 38 (1975), 54

143 Mountsandel Fort (C853307)

Location: 1¼ miles (2km) south-south-east of Coleraine, on the east bank of the River Bann in a forestry plantation, approached on foot by a forest path either from north or south. To appreciate its imposing command of the river, it can be viewed from the river walk on the opposite side of the Bann. The large oval mound, with its formidable deep ditch, dominates the river and was clearly of great strategic importance, but its date

Mountsandel Fort

remains something of a puzzle. Recent excavation in its vicinity has found nothing to support the traditional association of the mound with *Dún dá beann*, an important Early Christian stronghold, but evidence of this tradition may survive in the archaeology of other parts of the site. It may be an earthwork fortification of the Anglo-Norman invasion period, perhaps the castle of *Cell-Santain* built by John de Courcy, according to the *Annals of Ulster*, in 1197. Excavation at the foot of the mound produced radiocarbon dates consistent with an Anglo-Norman origin for the ditch. The features on the mound's summit are difficult to interpret but a ring-work or motte and bailey have both been suggested. The earthwork may have been used or modified for artillery warfare in the late 16th century or later.

McNeill 1980, 6, 103 and fig. 2; A.E.P. Collins in *Ulster J. Archaeol.* 46 (1983), 1–22; Woodman 1983, 193–198

144 O'Cahan's Castle (C679203)

Location: In the Roe Valley Country Park, south of the main car park. Very little survives of the original castle, marked now by a small mound on a defensive position high above the River Roe. The Thomas Raven map of 1622 shows a tower-house which Sir Thomas Phillips adapted with the addition of an artillery fort, but the narrow confines of the site indicate it was small. Behind the castle the drawing shows a walled garden in three parts, very like the one at Dunluce Castle.

Stevens Curl 1986, 432–433

145 Tullyheran Fort (C835017)

Location: 1¼ miles (2km) north-west of Maghera on the summit of a low hill in farmland. The ground slopes to the east and there are wide views to the south and east. This well-preserved rath has a substantial inner bank enclosing the level interior, a wide ditch and an outer (counterscarp) bank with an entrance gap to the south-east.

County Londonderry
Plantation Period and Later Monuments

146 Bellaghy Bawn (H953963)

Location: 4 miles (6.4km) north-west of Toome, approached on the A6 road from Toome to Londonderry and the B182 north to Bellaghy. The bawn stands on a height at the south end of the village and there is a small car park at its entrance. When this area was granted to the Vintners' Company of London in 1619, Sir Baptist Jones rented the land and built the bawn and the accompanying village to secure the region. This is now a complex, multi-period monument. The main house was lived in until as recently as 1987, and excavation in 1989–1990 clarified some of the site's complicated development.

Bellaghy Bawn

The north bawn wall with the entrance has disappeared, but parts of the other walls survive. The house was largely rebuilt in 1791 on the site of the original early 17th-century house, and the excavated foundations of another 17th-century house can be seen against the west bawn wall. A 1622 drawing by Thomas Raven shows two large round towers at opposed north-west and south-east corners of the bawn with splendid onion domes. The south-east one survives (with a less flamboyant roof), attached to the house and a mound indicates where the north-west one stood. On the surviving tower one can still see the outline of crenellations marking the original height. A gateway in the west wall leads through an earth rampart to the outside of the bawn revetted with stone where

County Londonderry
Plantation Period and Later Monuments

recent brick buttresses are the latest in a long series of attempts to prop the leaning wall. Excavation showed it had been built over the ditch of a rath of the Early Christian period, also exploiting this strategic spot, and explaining the instability. On the south-west corner is a small brick tower accessible from the rampart. This tower is an 18th-century replacement for the one in the Raven drawing. On the outside of the east bawn wall are two 18th-century houses, both worthy of note and to the south of the bawn, a garden terrace and a row of 18th- or 19th-century outhouses are also attractive. From this back yard the brick vault under the round tower can be entered.

In the house are historical and other displays featuring the work of Ulster poets, especially Seamus Heaney, who comes from this area. The resources include a film made for the bawn and a collection of Seamus Heaney's broadcasts. The materials are available for study and the building is often used for meetings and other events.

When looking at the village from the house today, no 17th-century buildings have survived but the house plots and church are still laid out as in the Raven drawing, and the stream is still visible north-west of the bawn.

E.M. Jope in *Ulster J. Archaeol.* 23 (1960), 108–109; Donnelly 1997, 116–118

---

147 Brackfield Bawn or Crossalt (C511097)

Brackfield Bawn

Location: 2¹/₂ miles (4km) north of Claudy, just north of the main A6 Londonderry road immediately south of Brackfield Presbyterian church. Large car park at entrance. The bawn, sited on a hillslope, commands the ancient east-west route to Londonderry, close to the Faughan River. It was built soon after 1611 by Sir Edward Doddington (see Dungiven Priory, 138) on land granted to the Skinners' Company and is shown in the drawing by Thomas Raven illustrating the 1622 survey compiled by Sir Thomas Phillips. The walled bawn is square with egg-shaped flanker towers at opposite (north-west and south-east) corners. The house along the south wall was 6m wide and its fireplaces can be seen, projecting beyond the line of the south wall. Excavation in 1983 confirmed the area of the house but little other information survived. There are gun-loops in the flankers.

E.M. Jope in *Ulster J. Archaeol.* 23 (1960), 113; N.F. Brannon in *Ulster J. Archaeol.* 53 (1990), 8–14

Location: The circuit of walls, enclosing the old city on the west bank of the River Foyle, is an impressive survival of 17th-century city walls roughly a mile in circumference. It has also been called 'the first major piece of urban planning in Ireland'. The city is built on a rocky hill, originally protected by the river to north and east and by a marsh, now the Bogside, to its west. The south west is the top of the hill.

During the 16th-century campaigns of Elizabeth I against the Gaelic lords of Ulster, Derry was a strategic location on the River Foyle for attacks on the O'Donnells of Donegal and the O'Neills of mid-Ulster. In May 1600 Sir Henry Docwra established a garrison at nearby Culmore Point and built earth ramparts to defend an area roughly half the size of the later walled town. In 1604, Derry was incorporated as a city with Docwra as its provost.

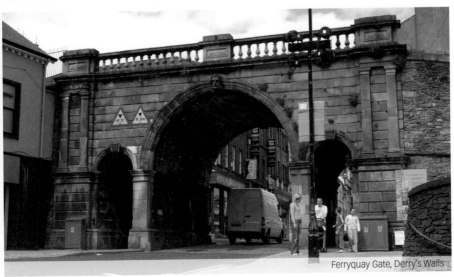
Ferryquay Gate, Derry's Walls

In 1608, however, O'Doherty of Donegal attacked and burnt Derry. As well as having the advantage of surprise, he benefited from the earth ramparts not being sufficiently strong for defence.

King James persuaded a reluctant group of London Guilds, named The Honourable the Irish Society, to invest in building a new town, renamed Londonderry in their honour, with more substantial defences, between 1613 and 1618. The walls underwent sieges in 1641, in 1648 and 1649, when the Parliamentarians held out against the Royalists and were relieved by General Owen Roe O'Neill. In 1688–1689 they withstood siege for 105 days against the forces of James II. The Honourable the Irish Society exists to this day.

County Londonderry
Plantation Period and Later Monuments

An earthen rampart was faced with stone, producing a wall 6m high and 5m wide, with a broad external ditch, now filled in. Five of the original eight artillery bastions survive and two shallow gun platforms. One of the missing bastions, Water Bastion, which was once washed by the Foyle, was excavated in 1983. Two watch-towers are preserved near St Columb's Cathedral but all four original gates have been changed: Bishop's Gate in 1789, commemorating the raising of the 1689 siege, and Butcher's, Ferryquay

Double Bastion

and Shipquay Gates in the 19th century. Three additional gates, Magazine, New and Castle Gates, are more recent. Many cannon are displayed on the north and west ramparts (40 originally defended the city). Steps and ramps lead to the wall-walk at several points inside the circuit.

Two walks are recommended. The first route begins on the wall-walk at the north-east beside Shipquay Gate and continues round in a clockwise direction. This gives the view of the defenders, protected by parapet and cannon. St Columb's Cathedral (1628–1633) in the south angle of the walls is one of the most remarkable buildings of the Ulster Plantation. There are fine views from the walls, a reminder of their original important strategic function. The second route runs round the outside. The most striking area is

Derry's Walls

between Ferry Bastion and Church Bastion where two stone watch towers defend the cathedral. A semicircular pedestrian gate in that wall, now blocked, was the original way for citizens to fetch water from a spring, The Fountain, after which this district is named. Several of the gates are fine examples of stonework, especially Bishop's Gate, built in 1789 on the centenary of the siege and intended originally to be crowned with a statue of William of Orange. It was designed by Henry Aaron Baker and has inlaid sculpture features by Edward Smyth, most notably keystones representing river gods, the Foyle and the Boyne, a match for the river gods on the Custom House in Dublin. Ferryquay Gate, built in 1866 is also impressive, enlarged to take the increase in traffic from the bridge.

Milligan 1948 and 1950; N.F. Brannon in *Ulster J. Archaeol.* 49 (1986), 93–95; Rowan 1979; Lacy 1988; Thomas 2005; Scott, 2008

149 Magilligan Martello Tower (C660388)

Magilligan Martello Tower

Location: In Doaghs Lower townland, 7 miles (11.2km) west-north-west of Castlerock, reached by the lane to Magilligan Point. Martello towers were built round the Irish and English coasts between 1804 and 1812 to guard against Napoleonic invasion. Magilligan tower, built in 1812, together with another at Greencastle on the Donegal coast opposite, commanded the strategically important entrance to Lough Foyle. The circular tower is built of dressed stone, 10m high, 12m in diameter, tapering slightly upwards. The entrance at first floor level was by retractable ladder and the five-corbelled machicolation above gave added protection. The ground floor was a powder and ammunition store with a water cistern, the first was residential, and on the top was a 24-pounder cannon on a central pivot and circular rail. A fireplace in the thickness of the wall top allowed the defenders to heat their ammunition – lethal against timber ships.

PLEASE NOTE: the tower is in Magilligan Nature Reserve. Visitors should take care not to stray onto the neighbouring army ranges.

Enoch 1978; Kerrigan 1995, 245 and 270–273

150 Tirkane Sweat House (C827025)

Tirkane Sweat House

Location: 2¹/₈ miles (3.4km) north-west of Maghera, ¹/₂ mile (0.8km) west of Killelagh Lough, reached by a long path west from a by-road, with a lay-by at the roadside. There are picnic tables at the site and there is a fine view. The sweat house is set into the side of a small, secluded leafy valley. Rectangular in plan, it is stone-built with a paved floor and lintelled roof. A small chimney hole allowed smoke to escape. The stone structure is covered with turf and looks externally like a grassy mound. The tradition was for people to use the sweat house in a group. It is difficult to date but an 18th-century date has been suggested. There is a small, cold, plunge pool nearby. Tirnony Dolmen (**130**) is 1 mile south-east.

PSAMNI 1940, 207; Weir 1980, 80–81 and 124

PREHISTORIC MONUMENTS

151. Balix Lower Court Tomb: The White Rocks (H483963)
152. Ballywholan Dual Court Tomb: Carnagat (H569470)
153. Ballywholan Portal Tomb: Carnfadrig (H555490)
154. Beaghmore Stone Circles, Cairns and Alignments (H685842)
155. Berrysfort Standing Stone (H272838)
156. Churchtown Wedge Tomb: Todd's Den (H268856)
157. Churchtown Portal Tomb: Druid's Altar (H266854)
158. Clogher Hillfort: Rathmore (H539513)
159. Copney Stone Circles (H599770)
160. Cregganconroe Court Tomb (H663758)
161. Creggandevesky Court Tomb (H646750)
162. Damphcloy Megalithic Structure (H595880)
163. Glenknock or Cloghogle Portal Tomb: Druid's Altar (H413879)
164. Grange Standing Stone (H832748)
165. Grange Standing Stones (H831751)
166. Killucan Wedge Tomb: Carnanbane (H683792)
167. Killucan Long Cairn: Killucan (H685801)
168. Knockmany Passage Tomb: Annia's Cove (H547559)
169. Lisky Court Tomb: Giant's Grave (H357905)
170. Tattykeel Standing Stone (H748774)

EARLY CHRISTIAN PERIOD MONUMENTS

171. Ardboe Cross and Abbey (H966756)
172. Donaghmore Cross (H768654)
173. Drumgormal Bivallate Rath (H873698)
174. Dungororan Rath (H739693)
175. Errigal Keerogue Cross and Church (H585570)
176. Killyliss Rath (H757605)
177. Tullaghoge Fort (H825743)

MEDIEVAL MONUMENTS

178. Harry Avery's Castle (H392852)
179. Magheraglass Church (H743768)
180. Mountjoy Castle (H901687)

PLANTATION PERIOD AND LATER MONUMENTS

181. Benburb or Wingfield's Castle (H814520)
182. Castle Caulfield (H755626)
183. Derryloran Church (H804768)
184. Moy Gates and Screen (H851560)
185. Newtownstewart Castle (H402858)
186. Reaskcor Tree-Ring (H749616)
187. Reaskmore Penal Altar Site (H754586)
188. Relignaman Women's Graveyard (H606722)
189. Roughan Castle (H823683)
190. Carrignahaltora (H578454)

County Tyrone
Prehistoric Monuments

---

151 Balix Lower Court Tomb: The White Rocks (H483963)

Location: 3 miles (4.8km) north of Plumbridge, high on the east-facing hillside overlooking Butterlope Glen, in rough pasture. The valley still forms an important north-south route through the Sperrins. This court tomb has a V-shaped forecourt at the uphill (west) end of a long cairn. An unusual feature is that the court springs from the jambs, rather than the jambs being within the curve of the court. This opens into a chamber, now undivided but perhaps originally divided into two parts. The cairn is much robbed but it may have been trapezoidal in shape.

PSAMNI 1940, 216; F. Lynch in *Ulster J. Archaeol.* 29 (1966), 39–42

---

152 Ballywholan Dual Court Tomb: Carnagat (H569470)

Location: 3¹/₂ miles (5.6km) south-east of Clogher, east of a minor road leading south off the B83, ¹/₂ mile (0.8km) from the Monaghan border, high in bogland overlooking the valley of the Fury river. This is a very well-preserved dual court tomb in a long cairn, orientated roughly north-east to south-west. A semicircular forecourt at each end leads to two-chambered galleries, back to back. The chambers are long and there are clear jamb stones separating the chambers and back stones terminating the galleries. The site was partly excavated in 1897. There were few finds but a leaf-shaped flint arrowhead is reported, as well as a possible stone wrist-guard or archer's bracer of the Bronze Age.

W. Wulff in *J. Roy. Soc. Antiq. Ireland* 52 (1922), 38–41; *PSAMNI* 1940, 259; D. Kelly in *J. Roy. Soc. Antiq. Ireland* 115 (1995), 162; Herity 1987, 245

---

153 Ballywholan Portal Tomb: Carnfadrig (H555490)

Location: 1¹/₂ miles (2.4km) north-west of Bellaghy Bawn (**146**), on a wooded hillslope north of the minor road which runs from the B83 south of Knockroe. A path leads from a small lay-by at the roadside. At the east end of a long, narrow, rectangular cairn is a large chamber made of three stones, entered between two portal stones (one leaning at an angle) and over a sill. At the west end are two chambers, set back-to-back and running north-south. Other settings of stones within the cairn are puzzling. They have been claimed to be further chambers, but the cairn is much disturbed and they may be the mutilated remains of structural features. This monument can be classified as a portal tomb, with subsidiary chambers. Like Carnagat (**152**), this cairn was partly excavated in 1897, when burned and unburned bone, pottery and flint implements were found. The name, Carnfadrig or Carnpatrick, comes from a traditional association with St Patrick, who was believed to have travelled along this valley from Armagh to visit St MacCairthinn at Clogher.

W. Wulff in *J. Roy. Soc. Antiq. Ireland* 53 (1923), 190–195 (note – the plan included in Wulff's paper is somewhat inaccurate); *PSAMNI* (1940), 258; Ó Nualláin 1983, 80, 89 and 103

154 Beaghmore Stone Circles, Cairns and Alignments (H685842)

Location: 8¹/₂ miles (13.6km) north-west of Cookstown, on the south-east fringes of the Sperrin Mountains, reached by minor roads north from the A505 Omagh road through Dunnamore, or from Draperstown south-west by the Six Towns road. There is a small car park at the site and a bigger one on the approach road from the south. A large, impressive series of Bronze Age ceremonial stone monuments was excavated from the surrounding bog between 1945 and 1949 and in 1965. The main features are the six stone circles (built of fairly small stones) occurring in pairs, with twelve small cairns which held cremation burials and stone rows all running in parallel suggesting a master plan. The 'Dragon's Teeth' is a single large circle filled with closely-set stones. Running under these features are low banks of small stones, probably derived from clearing fields for arable farming in Neolithic times. The stone structures continue to the north, under the bog,

Beaghmore Stone Circles, Cairns and Alignments

County Tyrone
Prehistoric Monuments

Beaghmore Stone Circles, Cairns and Alignments

and there are many other Neolithic and Bronze Age monuments in this area. Finds were sparse from the excavations but two flint hoards were found, one dated by radiocarbon to the late Neolithic and the other to the early Bronze Age. Study of pollen from a nearby former lake suggests Neolithic activity from 3500 BC, with the main period of the stone monuments in the Bronze Age, 1500 to 800 BC. See also Copney Stone Circles (**159**).

A. McL May in *J. Roy. Soc. Antiq. Ireland* 83 (1953), 174–197; J.R. Pilcher in *Ulster J. Archaeol.* 32 (1969), 73–91, and 38 (1975), 83–84; A.S. Burl in *Ulster J. Archaeol.* 43 (1980), 15–19; Donnelly 1997, 31–32

---

155 Berrysfort Standing Stone (H272838)

Berrysfort Standing Stone

Location: ²/₃ mile (1.1km) south-east of Castlederg, approached by farm lanes and across a field. This tall (2.3m-high), shapely pillar stands on a small eminence, just south of the River Derg.

156 Churchtown Wedge Tomb: Todd's Den (H268856)

Location: ³/₄ mile (1.2km) north-north-east of Castlederg, reached by a farm track east of the minor road which runs north-north-east from Castlederg to the Donegal border. No established access. This megalithic tomb seems to be largely intact under its covering cairn, and large capstones are visible. It is best regarded as a wedge tomb.

PSAMNI (1940), 220

157 Churchtown Portal Tomb: Druid's Altar (H266854)

Churchtown Portal Tomb

Location: ¹/₂ mile (0.8km) north-north-east of Castlederg, on rising ground overlooking the valley of the River Derg, east of the same minor road as **150**. A single chambered tomb, of massive stones, with two portal stones (one fallen) and a sill at the south end, one capstone in place and another collapsed. It is partly incorporated into a field wall.

PSAMNI 1940, 220; Ó Nualláin 1983, 79 and 101

158 Clogher Hillfort: Rathmore (H539513)

Location: On the prominent wooded hill on the south-west edge of Clogher, approached from the main A4 road by the lane along the cathedral graveyard wall to the south-east. A magnificent complex of earthworks crowns this hilltop, spanning the long period from the late Bronze Age to the 9th century AD. The location of this monument is very important, dominating the vital route through the Clogher valley between mountain ranges. Excavation between 1969 and 1977 suggested an enclosure of the late Bronze Age, but no sign of this appears above ground. In the Iron Age the hilltop was enclosed with a roughly rectangular earthwork, which enclosed an earlier, small ring-barrow at the south end of the site. In the late 6th century AD, when this was the royal centre of the Uí Chremthainn, rulers of the kingdom of Airgialla, the site was remodelled with the building of the substantial circular earthwork, still visible, on the highest part of the hill. Other features include the complex, probably multi-period earthworks at the north approach to the hill, the triangular mound at the south end, interpreted as a ceremonial or inauguration site, and a double-banked droveway running off to the south east, outside the area in state care. Finds from the excavation confirm the importance of the people

County Tyrone
Prehistoric Monuments

Clogher Hillfort

who lived here. They include pottery imported from the Mediterranean and France and the remains of fine bronze-working activity. After the 8th century this was no longer a royal headquarters and the site may have been abandoned in the 9th century.

The cathedral on the nearby ridge is the site of an important early church under the patronage of the neighbouring rulers. A visit to its graveyard is recommended to see the stone crosses, the gravestones, and the sundial in the porch, and to look back at the fort on the hill.

Warner 2000, 39–54

159 Copney Stone Circles (H599770)

Location: 10 miles (16km) east-north-east of Omagh, and 2 miles (3.2km) west-south-west of Creggan, approached from the A505 by a minor road to the south-west. This important complex of stone circles is on the north slope of Copney Hill, in the south foothills of the Sperrins, and was brought to notice only in 1979. The monuments extend down the slope for at least 180m, still partly covered by peat. The cut-over surface makes access difficult and the hillside is often very wet. Nine circles, a cairn and an alignment are visible, though there could be other features still under the bog. A tall standing stone on higher ground to the south, the highest stone on the site, overlooks the circles. The largest circles are at the top of the slope (north-west) and a double alignment links two of them. In 1994 these large circles were partly cleared of peat and were found to contain complex patterns of smaller stones, in one case a radial arrangement and in the other two concentric rings. Their central, probably burial, cairns had all been disturbed in antiquity. These newly uncovered stones stood out in dramatic white against the dark bog, but their surfaces were unstable and further uncovering was not attempted.

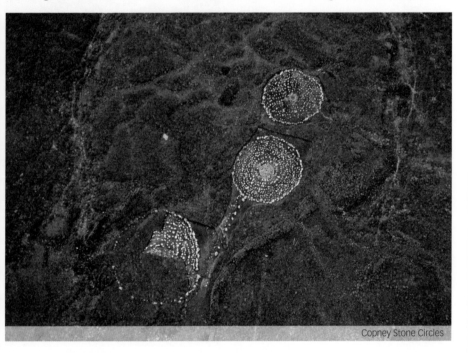

Copney Stone Circles

Down the slope, to the south-east, are the smaller circles, in at least one case forming a pair. After the clearance work, the Copney site was described as the most complex and visually impressive group of stone circles yet identified. They belong to the same mid-Ulster group as the Drumskinny (**110**) and Beaghmore (**154**) stone circles.

C. Foley in *Ulster J. Archaeol.* 46 (1983), 146–148; C. Foley and M. MacDonagh in *Archaeol. Ireland* 43 (1998), 24–28

County Tyrone
Prehistoric Monuments

160 Creganconroe Court Tomb (H663758)

Location: 3 miles (4.8km) north-west of Pomeroy, ½ mile (0.8km) south-south-west of Cam Lough, reached either from the north-east on a lane from the minor road west of Cam Lough, or by a lane from the east, past the farmhouse. This well-preserved court tomb stands on a prominent height in an area of sand and gravel ridges. A shallow forecourt at the east end opens

Cregganconroe Court Tomb

between tall portal stones (blocked by a fallen lintel) into a two-chamber burial gallery. One huge slipped capstone survives. Further west in the rectangular cairn are two small lateral chambers, originally reached between portal stones from the long sides of the cairn. The site has not been excavated, in contrast to nearby Creggandevesky (**161**).

PSAMNI 1940, 237

161 Creggandevesky Court Tomb (H646750)

Location: 2½ miles (4km) north-east of Carrickmore, prominently sited on a glacial hill at the west side of Lough Mallon. The recommended approach is on foot, round the south shore of the lough by the path, which leads off the minor road running north-west from the B4 west of Pomeroy towards Creggan. This very impressive court

Creggandevesky Court Tomb

tomb was a peat-covered, largely featureless mound and was threatened with removal in an agricultural reclamation scheme. When excavated between 1979 and 1982, it proved to be in an almost perfect state of preservation, and the owner agreed to its conservation and public access.

A semicircular forecourt at the south-east end leads to three burial chambers in a short trapezoidal cairn of granite boulders. The largest stone is a massive lintel over the entrance between the forecourt and the chambers. The cairn's drystone side revetment walls still stand to some height and some of the corbel stones of the roof are still in place. Thin sandstone slabs found inside the chambers suggest that the roof was completed with these finer stones. Cremated bone representing the remains of at least 21 people, flint implements and Neolithic pottery were found during the excavation, some of the material in the court area. Radiocarbon determinations suggest a date of about 3500 BC, but there were also signs of later, Bronze Age, activity in the court and at the back of the cairn.

PSAMNI 1940, 238; *PoP* 1988, 3–5; Donnelly 1997, 15–16

162 Damphcloy Megalithic Structure (H595880)

Location: In Crockatanty townland, 6¹/₂ miles (10.4km) east-north-east of Gortin, remotely sited and difficult to reach, high on the east side of Greenan Hill, overlooking the valleys of the Owenkillew and its tributary, the Coneyglen Burn. A huge rectangular boulder is supported at one side by the hillside and at the other by smaller boulders. This has

Damphcloy Megalithic Structure

been claimed to be a megalithic tomb, but there must be doubt about its antiquity. It could have been created by hollowing out loose material from under the 'capstone', and it may have been a shelter on the mountainside.

PSAMNI 1940, 224

163 Glenknock or Cloghogle Portal Tomb: Druid's Altar (H413879)

Location 1¹/₂ miles (2.4km) north-north-east of Newtownstewart, east of the minor road leading north off the B46 (Plumbridge) road at St Eugene's Church. The megalith is disturbed, but among the leaning stones it is possible to detect two portal stones at the north-west and a back stone. The capstone is shattered into five pieces and there are many field stones now set at the monument.

Glenknock or Cloghogle Portal Tomb

PSAMNI 1940, 221; Ó Nualláin 1983, 79 and 101

County Tyrone
Prehistoric Monuments

---

164 Grange Standing Stone (H832748)

Location: 2¹/₄ miles (3.6km) south-east of Cookstown, south of the hamlet of Grange, approached from the north along the side of a small graveyard and along the field boundary. This is a single, rather squat, standing stone.

165 Grange Standing Stones (H831751)

In a field north of Grange hamlet, this is a pair of standing stones set about 6m apart.

PSAMNI 1940, 240

166 Killucan Wedge Tomb: Carnanbane (H683792)

Grange Standing Stones

Location: 7³/₄ miles (12.4km) west of Cookstown and south of Dunnamore, ¹/₂ mile (0.8km) south of the main A505 Cookstown to Omagh road, on the edge of a valley with ground rising to the south. A roughly circular cairn is badly disturbed and is augmented with field stones. There are traces of a possible entrance to the south-west and of a burial gallery, suggesting a wedge tomb, but a mutilated court tomb has also been suggested.

PSAMNI 1940, 233; J.X.W.P. Corcoran in *Proc. Prehist. Soc.* 25 (1960), 143

167 Killucan Long Cairn: Killucan (H685801)

Location: north of (**166**), ¹/₈ mile (0.2km) south of the A505. This may have been a court tomb but it survives only as a badly mutilated and confused long, east-west cairn. There is one large capstone and a few other stones may be *in situ* at the east end. Not all authorities believe it is a megalithic tomb, and excavation would be needed to resolve the issue.

PSAMNI 1940, 233

168 Knockmany Passage Tomb: Annia's Cove (H547559)

Location: 1³/₄ miles (2.8km) north-west of Augher, approached from Augher or Clogher, on the summit of Knockmany in the Forest Park, reached by an uphill path through the forest from the car park on the north-west side of the hill. The cairn commands superb views south over the Clogher Valley. The covering cairn in its present form is modern, added in 1959 to protect the stones from weathering and vandalism. Excavation showed that a stone cairn capped with earth within a stone revetment originally covered the burial chamber. The passage of the 'classic' passage tomb is absent but several of the stones forming the chamber are decorated with characteristic passage tomb art, including circles, spirals and zigzags. One of the best examples of this art is in the north. There is access to the mound at all times, and a general view of the stones can be had through the gate of the chamber, but there is no regular arrangement for unlocking the chamber. Prospective visitors who wish to examine the stones in detail should contact NIEA to arrange for the chamber to be opened.

Knockmany Passage Tomb

A.E.P. Collins and D.M. Waterman in *Ulster J. Archaeol.* 15 (1952), 26–30; A.E.P. Collins and H.A. Meek in *Ulster J. Archaeol.* 23 (1960), 2–8; Donnelly 1997, 18–20; Foley 2000, 15–17

169 Lisky Court Tomb: Giant's Grave (H357905)

Location: 2 miles (3.2km) south-east of Sion Mills, south of the B165 Strabane to Newtownstewart road, on a rocky outcrop on the north bank of the River Mourne. Six very large stones make up a long chamber running east-west, with a low sill stone to the west and a back stone to the east. These are probably the remains of a court tomb. Large stones in the vicinity may come from other chambers or from a court, but without excavation the original form is uncertain.

PSAMNI 1940, 217

170 Tattykeel Standing Stone (H748774)

Location: 4 miles (6.4km) west of Cookstown, south of the main A505 Cookstown to Omagh road and east of a farm track. This single shapely standing stone stands 2.15m high.

Tattykeel Standing Stone

County Tyrone
Early Christian Period Monuments

171 Ardboe Cross and Abbey (H966756)

Location: In Farsnagh and Sessia townlands, 5 miles (8km) east-south-east of Coagh, reached by turning south off the B73, on a promontory on the west shore of Lough Neagh. The tall cross marks the area of an ecclesiastical site associated with St Colman, founded in the 6th or 7th century. Ardboe was burned in 1166 but later emerged as a medieval parish church site. The cross is the finest of the Ulster figure-carved crosses, despite damage and weathering, with an exceptionally full scheme of biblical carving. On the east (Old Testament) side are Adam and Eve, the sacrifice of Isaac, Daniel between lions, the three children in the fiery furnace, a figure with bell and crosier surrounded by people, and Christ in glory or the last judgement, with scales and flames beneath.

Ardboe Cross and Abbey

The west (New Testament) side has the visit of the Magi, the miracle at Cana, the multiplication of loaves and fishes, the entry to Jerusalem, the arrest or the flagellation of Christ, and the crucifixion. On the south side are Cain and Abel, David struggling with the lion, David killing Goliath, and the raven feeding Paul and Anthony in the Egyptian desert. The scenes on the north side are less easy to interpret but the baptism, the judgment of Solomon, the slaughter of the innocents and the annunciation to the shepherds have all been suggested. A 10th-century date is likely for the cross.

Ardboe 'Abbey' is a small, featureless ruin in the field north of the graveyard, impossible to date. The ruined church in the graveyard (not in state care) lacks distinctive features but is probably of the early 17th century. At the west end of the graveyard are the remains of two spear-shaped bastions, surviving from an artillery fort, probably created here when Sir Arthur Chichester secured the west shore of Lough Neagh at the beginning of the 17th century.

F.J. Bigger and W.J. Fennell in *Ulster J. Archaeol.* 4 (1897–8), 1–6; *PSAMNI* 1940, 241–242; H. Roe in *Seanchas Ardmhacha* 2 no. 1 (1956), 81–83; Harbison 1990, 15–18 and figs 30–41; Donnelly 1997, 59–61. The cross is a prominent character in Polly Devlin's *All of us there* (1983) and *The far side of the Lough* (1983)

172 Donaghmore Cross (H768654)

Donaghmore Cross

Location: 2¹/₂ miles (4km) north-west of Dungannon, at the busy road junction at the west end of Donaghmore's main street, outside the old graveyard. This sandstone cross survives from an early church on or near its present site, traditionally founded by St Patrick, who left the priest Colum there with book and bell. An Early Christian bronze bell associated with Donaghmore parish, known as the Bell of Clogher, is in the National Museum, Dublin. The church later became a parish church. The present cross is made up of parts of two different crosses, the base and lower shaft not quite matching the upper shaft and head. It is known to have been thrown down in the 17th century and re-erected in the 18th century. Its decoration includes an interesting mixture of figure-carving and motifs in distinctive circular, diamond-shaped and semicircular frames. On the east side are the annunciation to the shepherds, the baptism, the adoration of the Magi, the miracle at Cana, the multiplication of loaves and fishes, the arrest or flagellation, and the crucifixion of Christ. On the west side are Adam and Eve, Cain and Abel and the sacrifice of Isaac. There is a horseman, perhaps unfinished, on the west side of the base. Like Ardboe cross (**171**), this one probably dates from the 10th century. In the adjacent graveyard is a fine bullaun stone, also many fine gravestones and a copy of the cross, made in 2000.

PSAMNI 1940, 245; H. Roe in *Seanchas Ardmhacha* 2 no. 1 (1956), 85–87; Brennan 1988; Harbison 1990, 64–67 and figs 191–200

County Tyrone
Early Christian Period Monuments

173 Drumgormal Bivallate Rath (H873698)

Location: 1¼ miles (2km) east-south-east of Stewartstown, and close to the south-west of Drumcairne Forest. This is a fine rath on a prominent hilltop, with extensive views in all directions. It was planted with trees as a landscape feature in the former estate of Drumcairne House. There is a low bank around the circular central area, which slopes slightly to the south. Next comes a deep ditch, then a second bank and an outer ditch, best preserved on the south side. The rath is approached from the north-east, but unfortunately public access is not presently secured.

174 Dungororan Rath (H739693)

Location: 5½ miles (8.8km) north-west of Dungannon, north-east of the B43 to Pomeroy, approached by narrow farm lanes. This platform rath is prominently sited on a glacial hilltop. It is circular with a considerably raised interior, with traces of a low perimeter bank on the north and a wide, wet surrounding ditch. No secure access.

175 Errigal Keerogue Cross and Church (H585570)

Location: In Gort townland, 2¾ miles (4.4km) west of Ballygawley, reached by minor roads north and north-west from the A4 Ballygawley to Clogher road. The ridge-top graveyard is beautifully sited overlooking the Clogher valley. An early church here was

Errigal Keerogue Cross and Church

associated with St Ciaran (Dachiarog), and the medieval parish church was also here. The cross west of the church has been called 'archaic' and 'primitive', but it is clearly unfinished. On the east face a ringed cross is lightly tooled; on the west a flat boss was worked and straight lines were marked out, but the stone was not further cut back, perhaps because of the flaw visible on the south side. Why an unfinished cross was retained and valued remains something of a mystery. The church shows signs of more than one period. It has opposed doors to north and south and a base batter on the east wall. Numerous querns and quern fragments have been found in the graveyard and a few are built for display into the north wall, together with a modern cast of a medieval burial monument found in the graveyard. St Kieran's Well is across the road to the north-east.

PSAMNI 1940, 254; H. Roe in *Seanchas Ardmhacha* 2 no. l (1956), 88; N.F. Brannon in *Ulster J. Archaeol.* 44–45 (1981–2), 200–202; Harbison 1990, 88 and figs 274–275

176 Killyliss Rath (H757605)

Location: 2³/₄ miles (4.4km) west-south-west of Dungannon, south of the summit of a small hill, with good views in all directions. It is approached from the north by minor roads from the A4 (old main road). This is a bivallate rath with a circular central area and a low, spread inner bank, surrounded by a ditch, a very substantial bank and a wide outer ditch. The entrance is on the south-east side. Small-scale excavation was

Killyliss Rath

done in 1965 when the site was threatened by the nearby motorway (its line was later moved). Hearths and material of the Early Christian period were found.

177 Tullaghoge Fort (H825743)

Location: In Ballymully Glebe townland, 2¹/₂ miles (4km) south-south-east of Cookstown, east of the B162 Cookstown to Stewartstown road. The entrance is on a difficult corner, with a small car park at the foot of the hill, from which an uphill path leads to the site. This magnificent hilltop enclosure commands wide views and, planted with trees, is visible from miles around. The site comes into historical prominence in the 11th century when it was a dynastic centre and inauguration place of the Cenél nEógain (later the O'Neills). It was the residence of the O'Hagans who, with the O'Cahans, performed the inauguration ceremony. The O'Hagan burial place, Donaghrisk, is the circular walled graveyard at the

County Tyrone
Early Christian Period Monuments

Tullaghoge Fort

foot of the hill to the south-west. The earthwork is not of classic rath form. It was not a defensive site, but rather a royal power centre. An inner polygonal embanked enclosure is separated from an outer bank by a wide, flat space, and there is no external ditch. The fort is shown in Bartlett's 1601 pictorial map with two gateways and two thatched buildings. The widow of the planter, Robert Lindsey, was living here in 1619,

Tullaghoge Fort

but the site was abandoned by 1622. The stone inauguration chair, visible on the 1601 map on the hillside to the south, was broken up by the English Lord Deputy Mountjoy, advancing north against the O'Neills in 1602.

PLEASE NOTE: as the entrance to this site is on a difficult corner, please take care when entering or leaving the car park.

Ulster J. Archaeol. 5 (1857), 235–242; Hayes-McCoy 1964, 8–9; G.A. Hayes-McCoy in *Ulster J. Archaeol.* 33 (1970), 89–94; Donnelly 1997, 74–77

County Tyrone
Medieval Monuments

178 Harry Avery's Castle (H392852)

Harry Avery's Castle

Location: ³/₄ mile (1.2km) South-west of Newtownstewart, in Upper New Deer Park Townland, approached across a field from the minor road to Rakelly. The castle stands on a prominent hill, commanding important river valley routes. It is named after Henry Aimhréidh O'Neill who died in 1392, and a late 14th-century date is possible (the excavation discovered a 14th-century window head). It is an unusual and interesting ruin, a stone castle deep in Gaelic Ulster. An artificially scarped natural mound formed an elevated 'bailey' or courtyard, surrounded by a polygonal curtain wall with at least two projecting towers, all now ruined to a low level. At its south-west end is a tower that looks like a gatehouse (Carrickfergus Castle for example or Criccieth in Wales), defended by a bridge-pit and entered between high D-shaped towers, but the only way into the courtyard behind was up a stair and through the hall at first floor level. In function the building resembles a tower-house rather than a true gatehouse. Features include a draw-bar slot for the main door, latrine chutes and marks of wicker centring in the tower vaults.

E.M. and H.M. Jope and E.A. Johnson in *Ulster J. Archaeol.* 13 (1951), 81–92; S.G. Rees-Jones and D.M. Waterman in *Ulster J. Archaeol.* 30 (1967), 76–82; Mallory and McNeill 1991, 272–273; Donnelly 1997, 95–97

179 Magheraglass Church (H743768)

Location: 4¹/₄ miles (6.8km) west-south-west of Cookstown, difficult to access across fields. The overgrown, low remains of a ruined medieval church stand on the site of a pre-Norman church, the west wall incorporated into a field boundary. An enclosure reported in the 19th century no longer exists above ground, although its line may be reflected in the raised oval area in which the church stands. One bullaun stone survives on site and a second is reported.

H.B. Carter in *J. Roy. Soc. Antiq. Ireland* 23 (1893), 84–86; *PSAMNI* (1940), 239

County Tyrone
Medieval Monuments

180 Mountjoy Castle (H901687)

Location: In Magheralamfield townland, 3 miles (4.8km) east-south-east of Stewartstown, reached by a lane west off the B161. Small car park at entrance. Standing on a low hill overlooking Lough Neagh, the castle is a small, early 17th-century campaign fort or blockhouse. The building is of stone below, with dressed quoins, and brick above, in parts badly weathered, especially inside. The central rectangular block has four spear-shaped angle towers with gun-loops for raking fire along the walls, but only three of the towers are accessible to visitors. The entrance was in the south-east wall, where a draw-bar hole

Mountjoy Castle

can be seen. This is probably the fortification reported in 1611 by Sir George Carew as having been built 'beside the old fort' and finished after 1605. It is not to be identified with the large fort built by Francis Roe during Mountjoy's northward advance against O'Neill in 1602 (the 'old fort') and illustrated in a pictorial map by Richard Bartlett. This was probably on land closer to the lough shore. The forts in this area continued in use to the late 17th century.

E.M. Jope in *Ulster J. Archaeol.* 23 (1960), 97–125, esp. 101; Hayes-McCoy 1964, 13

County Tyrone
Plantation Period and Later Monuments

---

181 Benburb or Wingfield's Castle (H814520)

Location: In the grounds of Benburb Servite Priory, approached on foot down the drive from the main street beyond (west of) the main Priory entrance. Dramatically sited on the cliff edge above the River Blackwater, this is a bawn built by Sir Richard Wingfield in about 1615, on or near the site of a stronghold of Shane O'Neill. The bawn walls enclose an irregular rectangular area, the walls standing almost to full height, plentifully supplied with gun-loops. At the north-east and north-west corners are rectangular towers, large, with fireplaces and more like tall houses than defensive flankers. The north-west tower has been re-roofed and restored. At the south end is a circular tower with a stair down to a postern gate at the cliff edge. The 19th-century house in the bawn is privately occupied and not accessible.

PSAMNI (1940), 257; O. Davies in *Ulster J. Archaeol.* 4 (1941), 31–34

Benburb or Wingfield's Castle

County Tyrone
Plantation Period and Later Monuments

Location: On the south-east edge of the village beside a stream are the substantial remains of an English-style house, built by Sir Toby Caulfield in around 1619 on the site of a fort of the O'Donnellys. The Caulfield arms appear over the gatehouse. This is vaulted with murder-holes and pistol-loops and, with a fragment of bawn wall, is earlier than the main house. The house was undefended, three storeys high with attics, and was originally of half H plan, but it is now L-shaped, lacking its north-west wing. There are many large

Castle Caulfield

windows and good cut stone details like string courses and chimneys. In the main block was a hall of medieval plan with opposed doorways and cellars under the south end, and the large windows in the north-east gable suggest that the most important chambers were there. The kitchen was in the north-east wing. The castle was burned by the O'Donnellys in 1641 but was repaired and reoccupied by the Caulfields. There are still signs of the burning and plentiful evidence of structural alterations following the 1641 attack. St Oliver Plunkett is known to have carried out ordinations in the castle courtyard, in 1670 when William Caulfield, 5th Lord and 1st Viscount was in residence but the building was disused by the end of the century. John Wesley preached in front of the gate in 1767.

The parish church in the village has fine carved stonework of the 17th century.

E.M. Jope in *Ulster J. Archaeol.* 21 (1958), 101–107

183 Derryloran Church (H804768)

Location: On the south-west edge of
Cookstown, in Glebe townland, beside
the Ballinderry River, close to a bridge
and on the A505 (Omagh) road. The
ruined church occupies the site of a
pre-Norman church associated with St
Luran. A church here was plundered in
1195 and the medieval parish church
was on this site. A 1622 survey reported
a church as 'almost finished' and the

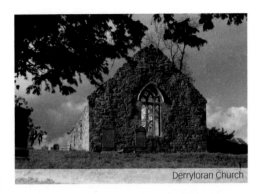
Derryloran Church

present ruin is largely of that church, though incorporating some earlier worked stones.
Excavation showed that it was built on the foundations of the medieval church, at least
at the east end. The church is a long, narrow structure, well supplied with windows,
including a three-light east window with uncusped intersecting tracery (partly restored).
Towards the west end the window details are different and it is likely that the church was
lengthened in the 18th century, when the porch and bell-cote were added and the grand
gateposts were provided. This building continued in use as the parish church long after
the development of Cookstown some distance away, but in 1822 it was abandoned for
the new church in the town. The graveyard continued in use for burials.

O. Davies in *Ulster J. Archaeol.* 5 (1942), 8–11; N.F. Brannon in *Ulster J. Archaeol.* 49 (1986),
95–98; Donnelly 1997, 109–111

184 Moy Gates and Screen (H851560)

Location: On the north side of the road at the east approach to the Moy on the A29,
these gates mark the entrance to the now-vanished Roxborough Castle. Between stone
end-pillars are curving screens, openwork columns, and pedestrian and carriage gates,
all of elaborate cast iron, the best surviving example of their type in Northern Ireland.
Their exact date is uncertain, but they may be the work of the celebrated Dublin iron-
founder, Richard Turner, who is known to have worked at Roxborough in the mid 19th
century. This cast ironwork should be contrasted with the wrought iron Richhill Gates at
Hillsborough (**104**).

County Tyrone
Plantation Period and Later Monuments

185 Newtownstewart Castle (H402858)

Newtownstewart Castle

Location: Prominently sited at the bottom of the main street, a striking feature here ever since the early 17th century. The castle stands at the top of a slope down to the River Strule, and is the third defensive site in this area, at the heart of O'Neill territory in the pre-Plantation period. The mound called Pigeon Hill in the recreation ground across the river to the east is the first, while Harry Avery's Castle (**178**) nearby was the medieval stronghold of the O'Neills. The place seems already to have been called 'new town' (*baile nua*) before the Plantation, but the present street plan survives from the early 17th century. The castle was built in about 1619 by Sir Robert Newcomen and was modified by his son-in-law, Sir William Stewart, after 1628.

The castle was rectangular with a thick central wall. It had three storeys above a basement but only its north and west walls and a little of the south survive. The most distinctive feature is the triple gables to the street, with the tall chimney-stack over the smaller centre gable. The stepped gables are a Scottish feature while the eight-pointed-star-shaped brick chimney-stack is derived from England. Half of a fine door survives near the south corner with a frustrating half date, 16.., on the remaining stone. Other

Newtownstewart Castle

features include the mullioned windows, clearly domestic and not defensive, fireplaces, a circular projecting stair tower, and a rectangular tower at the north-east corner, perhaps a flanker tower on the bawn wall. On the main front there are doorways on all three floors with the scar of stairs leading to the doors. This indicates a building which would have blocked a strip of the façade – either a timber stair turret, or possibly a service block. Another possibility is that the house divided into two separate residences.

The castle was burned by Sir Phelim O'Neill in 1641 and again by King James in 1689, on his retreat from Londonderry. The fine 19th-century arcade in the middle of the house belongs to the corn exchange, part of the local market that used three yards in a row, the castle, the inn and the town hall. In recent years the castle has been disentangled from a shop built onto the gable, and excavation in conjunction with conservation in the late 1990s has revealed more of its plan and, most unexpectedly, found a two-segment Bronze Age cist with cremation burials and pottery south-west of the castle, attesting to very early activity on this site above the river.

H. Meek and E.M. Jope in *Ulster J. Archaeol.* 21 (1958), 109–112

186 Reaskcor Tree-Ring (H749616)

Location: 3 miles (4.8km) west-south-west of Dungannon, north of the A4, on a prominent hilltop with fine views. Though the spot is known as Fort Hill, this enclosure is not an Early Christian period rath but a 'tree-ring', a domed circular area surrounded by a fairly slight circular bank in which trees were planted, made probably in the 18th century as a landscape feature for Parkanaur House to the west. Most of the old trees have been felled here, but there are several other hilltop tree-rings in the area which retain their trees.

B.B. Williams in *Ulster J. Archaeol.* 43 (1980), 97–101 on tree-rings

187 Reaskmore Penal Altar Site (H754586)

Location: 3½ miles (5.6km) south-west of Dungannon. This was a small, secluded space where Mass was celebrated during Penal times. The site is at the base of a south-east-facing slope, a shallow scoop with trees, left uncultivated in otherwise cultivated ground. No stone altar survives.

188 Relignaman Women's Graveyard (H606722)

Location: ½ mile (0.8km) south-west of Carrickmore, on a rocky height in a landscape much altered by quarrying. A small, irregularly-shaped enclosure has a grass-grown tumbled wall and small, uninscribed stones and mounds marking graves. Traditionally only women were buried here: no dead man or living woman was meant to enter the enclosure. The monument in its present form is impossible to date closely (hence its inclusion in this section) but the use of the site may be very ancient. There was a pre-Norman church at Carrickmore and traditionally Relignaman (which means 'the women's graveyard') originated from St Columba's insistence that a wicked woman should be buried out of earshot of his bell. At Carrickmore there were also special burial grounds for children and for people who had died violently.

G. Gillespie in *J. Roy. Soc. Antiq. Ireland* 66 (1936), 295–311; A. Hamlin and C. Foley in *Ulster J. Archaeol.* 46 (1983), 41–46; Hamlin 2000, 102–104

County Tyrone
Plantation Period and Later Monuments

Location: 1½ miles (2.4km) north-west of Coalisland and 2½ miles (4km) south-west of Stewartstown, best approached by the minor road that runs from Newmills, along the north-west shore of Roughan Lough towards Stewartstown. Park on the road and walk along a path to the castle, which is on a lawn in front of Roughan House. This impressive castle was built in 1618 by Sir Andrew Stewart, after whom nearby Stewartstown is named. Its plan is unusual among Plantation castles, with a central, three-storey square block and four sturdy circular towers at the corners. Cut-stone string courses outside

Roughan Castle

indicate the floors inside and there are simple small windows at the higher levels. On the south side a high arch supported on corbels links the two towers, like an earlier defensive machicolation, but here not protecting the door and probably for show. There are gun-loops in the towers at ground floor level and on the south-west tower the scar of the lost bawn wall can be seen. The castle was entered through the north-west tower, which also accommodated the spiral stair. The south-east tower is vaulted at ground floor level and fireplaces survive in the north wall. The floors were made of wood, but it is not clear how this unusual castle was roofed. The crannóg visible in Roughan Lough to the north-east was described as 'O'Neill's strongest island fort' at the beginning of the 17th century, and Sir Phelim O'Neill was captured there in 1653.

Earl of Belmore in *Ulster J. Archaeol.* 10 (1904), 95–96; *PSAMNI* (1940), 244–245; *AMNI* (1969), 31–32 and pl. 8b

190 Carrignahaltora (H578454)

Location: 4½ miles (7.2km) south of Clogher 3½ miles (5.75km) east of summit of Slieve Beagh. No public access as the monument is situated in upland bog. The site is situated on a high drumlin overlooking the Co. Monaghan border which is some 100m to the south and consists of a settlement of three hut sites, probably booley huts (a kind of seasonal settlement in upland zones), each of which are rectangular, drystone foundations. Two of the three examples are built in shallow scoops which have been dug into the hillside. There is some suggestion that this site was used for Mass during Penal Times – the Irish name Carricknahaltora means 'rock of the altar'. No obvious stone altar survives, though this may have been a temporary structure.

Bibliography/Abbreviations
used in the inventory

AMNI 1969 *Ancient Monuments of Northern Ireland: not in State Care*, (HMSO, Belfast, 1969) 31–32 and pl. 8b

ASCD 1966: *An archaeological survey of County Down* (HMSO, Belfast, 1966)

Archaeol. Ireland: *Archaeology Ireland*

Archaeol. Newsletter: *Archaeology Newsletter*

Atkinson 1925: E.D. Atkinson, *Dromore: an Ulster Diocese* (Dundalk, 1925), 87–89;

Blair 1981: M. Blair *Once Upon the Lagan* (1981) 9–12

Brennan 1988: E. Brennan, *Impressions of a cross: Donaghmore, County Tyrone* (Dungannon, 1988)

Brett 1996: C.E.B. Brett, *Buildings of County Antrim* (Belfast, 1996)

Brett 1999: C.E.B. Brett, *Buildings of County Armagh* (Belfast, 1999)

Butler 1992: J. Butler in *The Buildings of Armagh,* R. McKinstry and others (eds) (UAHS, Belfast, 1992), 24–26

CAF DSR No. 44: Centre of Archaeological Fieldwork *Data Structure Report No. 44 Excavations at St. Patricks Church, Armoy, Co. Antrim* www.qub.ac.uk/schools/CentreforArchaeologicalFieldworkCAF/

Collins, Waterman and others 1955: A.E.P. Collins, D.M. Waterman and others, *Millin Bay, a late Neolithic cairn in county Down* (HMSO, 1955)

Co. Louth Archaeol. J: *Journal of the County Louth Archaeological Society*

Cooney 2000: G. Cooney, *Landscapes of the Neolithic* (London, 2000), 99–103

Day and McWilliams 1992: A. Day and P. McWilliams, *Ordnance Survey Memoirs of Ireland: Parishes of Antrim V*, vol. 16 (Belfast, 1992), 106 and 116

Day, McWilliams and Dobson 1994: A. Day, P. McWilliams and N. Dobson (eds), *Ordnance Survey Memoirs of Ireland: Parishes of Londonderry VII,* 1834–5, vol. 25 (Belfast, 1994), 10

Dixon 1975: H. Dixon, *An introduction to Ulster architecture* (UAHS, Belfast, 1975), 18

DOENI guide-card 1991: Department of the Environment for Northern Ireland guide-card (1991)

DOENI guide-card 1992: Department of the Environment for Northern Ireland guide-card (1992)

DOENI guide book 1993: Department of the Environment for Northern Ireland Guide Book (1993)

DOENI guide-card 1997: Department of the Environment for Northern Ireland guide-card 1997

DOENI guide book 1998: Department of the Environment for Northern Ireland Guide Book (1998)

DOENI leaflet 1998: *1798 Rebellion in Ulster,* Department of the Environment for Northern Ireland leaflet (1998)

Donnelly 1997: C.J. Donnelly, *Living places: archaeology, continuity and change at historic monuments in Northern Ireland* (Belfast, 1997)

Enoch 1978: V.J. Enoch, *The Martello towers of Ireland* (1978)

Evans 1966: E. Evans, *Prehistoric and Early Christian Ireland: a guide* (London, 1966)

Foley 2000: C. Foley in *Tyrone: history and society,* C. Dillon and H.A. Jefferies (eds) (Dublin, 2000), 15–17

Green 1963: E.R.R. Green, *The Industrial Archaeology of County Down* (HMSO, 1963), 80 and pl. 32

Gwynn and Hadcock 1970: A. Gwynn and R.N. Hadcock, *Medieval religious houses: Ireland* (London, 1970)

Hamlin 1995: A. Hamlin in *From the Isles of the North,* C. Bourke (ed.) (Belfast, 1995), 187–196

Bibliography/Abbreviations used in the inventory

Hamlin 2000: A. Hamlin in *Tyrone: history and society,* C. Dillon and H.A. Jefferies (eds) (Dublin, 2000), 102–104

Hamlin 2001: A. Hamlin in *Ogma,* J-M Picard and M. Richter (eds) (Dublin, 2001)

Harbison 1990: P. Harbison, *The high crosses of Ireland,* 3 vols (Bonn, 1990)

Hartwell 1998: B. Hartwell, 'The Ballynahatty complex' in *Prehistoric ritual and religion,* A. Gibson and D. Simpson (eds) (Stroud, 1998), 32–44

Hayes-McCoy 1964: G.A. Hayes-McCoy, *Ulster and other Irish maps c. 1600* (Dublin, 1964)

Herity 1987: M. Herity, 'The finds from Irish court tombs', *Proc. Roy. Irish Acad* 87C (1987), 103–281

Hickey 1985: H. Hickey, *Images of stone: figure sculpture of the Erne basin* (Fermanagh, 1985)

J. Roy. Soc. Antiq. Ireland: Journal of the Royal Society of Antiquaries of Ireland

Kerrigan 1995: Paul M. Kerrigan *Castles and Fortifications in Ireland, 1485–1945* (Cork, 1995) 267–269

Lacy 1988: B. Lacy, *Historic Derry* (Belfast, 1988)

Lalor 1999: B. Lalor, *The Irish round tower: origins and architecture explored* (Cork, 1999)

Lanigan Wood 1990: H. Lanigan Wood, *Enniskillen: historic images of an island town* (Belfast, 1990)

Lawlor 1925: H.C. Lawlor *The monastery of St. Mochaoi of Nendrum* (Belfast, 1925)

Lisburn Hist. Soc. J.: Lisburn Historical Society Journal

Macalister 1945: R.A.S. Macalister, *Corpus Inscriptionum Insularum Celticarum* (Dublin, 1945), 304

Mallory and McNeill 1991: J.P. Mallory and T.E. McNeill, *The archaeology of Ulster from colonization to plantation* (Belfast, 1991)

McCutcheon 1980: W.A. McCutcheon, *The industrial archaeology of Northern Ireland* (HMSO, Belfast, 1980)

McErlean, McConkey and Forsythe, 2002: T. McErlean, R. McConkey, and W. Forsythe, *Strangford Lough: An Archaeological Survey of the Maritime Cultural Landscape* (Belfast 2002)

McErlean and Crothers, 2007: T. McErlean and N. Crothers, *Harnessing the Tides: The Early Medieval Tide Mills at Nendrum* (Belfast, 2007)

McNab 1987: S. McNab in *New perspectives: studies in art history,* J. Fenlon, N. Figgis and C. Marshall (eds) (Dublin, 1987), 19–33

McNeill 1997: T. McNeill, *Castles in Ireland: feudal power in a Gaelic world* (London, 1997)

McNeill 1980: T.E. McNeill, *Anglo-Norman Ulster* (Edinburgh, 1980), 6, 103 and fig. 2

McNeill 1981: T.E. McNeill, *Carrickfergus Castle* (DOENI monograph, Belfast, 1981)

Milligan 1948 and 1950: C.D. Milligan, *The Walls of Derry, their building, defending and preserving,* 2 vols (Londonderry, 1948 and 1950)

Neill 1999: K. Neill in *Derry and Londonderry: history and society,* G. O'Brien (ed.) (Dublin, 1999), 63–64

Ó Baoill 2008: R. Ó Baoill, *Carrickfergus: The Story of a Castle & Walled Town* (Belfast, 2008)

Ó Nualláin 1983: S. Ó Nualláin, 'Irish portal tombs: topography, siting and distribution', *J. Roy. Soc. Antiq. Ireland* 113 (1983), 75–105

PoP 1988: A. Hamlin and C. Lynn (eds), *Pieces of the past: archaeological excavations by the Department of the Environment for Northern Ireland 1970–1986* (HMSO, Belfast, 1988)

PSAMNI 1940: *A preliminary survey of the ancient monuments of Northern Ireland* (HMSO, Belfast, 1940)

Proc. Belfast Nat. Hist. Phil. Soc.: Proceedings of the Belfast Natural History and philosophical Society.

Bibliography/Abbreviations
used in the inventory

Proc. Prehist. Soc.: Proceedings of the Prehistoric Society

Proc. Roy. Irish Acad.: Proceedings of the Royal Irish Academy

Reeves 1847: W. Reeves, Ecclesiastical antiquities of Down, Connor and Dromore (Dublin, 1847), 9–10

Rowan 1979: A. Rowan, Northwest Ulster, (Frome 1979)

Scott, 2008: B.G. Scott, R.R. Brown, A.G. Leacock, and C.J. Salter, The Great Guns Like Thunder; The Cannon from Derry (Derry, 2008)

Stalley 1987: R. Stalley, The Cistercian monasteries of Ireland (London, 1987), 245 and elsewhere

Stevens Curl 1986: James Stevens Curl, The Londonderry Plantation 1609–1914, (Chichester, 1986) 432–433

Thomas 2005: A. Thomas, Irish Historic Towns Atlas No. 15 Derry – Londonderry (Dublin 2005)

Ulster J. Archaeol.: Ulster Journal of Archaeology

Warner 2000: R. Warner in Tyrone: history and society, C. Dillon and H.A. Jefferies (eds) (Dublin, 2000), 39–54

Waterman 1997: D.M. Waterman, Excavations at Navan Fort 1961–71 (ed. C.J. Lynn) (DOENI monograph, Belfast, 1997)

Weir 1980: A. Weir, Early Ireland: a field guide (Belfast, 1980), 80–81 and 124

Woodman 1983: P.C. Woodman, Excavations at Mount Sandel 1973–77 (DOENI monograph, Belfast, 1983)

Notes

Notes